How to Keep
SOFTBIL
in Cage or Aviary

C000135409

RICHARD MARK MARTIN

with illustrations by Michael Stringer

John Bartholomew & Son Ltd
Edinburgh

First published in Great Britain 1980 by
John Bartholomew & Son Limited,
12 Duncan Street, Edinburgh EH9 1TA

© John Bartholomew & Son Limited, 1980

Front cover illustration:
Spreo starling (left) Golden-Fronted fruitsucker (right)

British Library Cataloguing in Publication Data

Martin, Richard Mark
 How to keep softbilled birds in cage or aviary.
 1. Cage-birds
 I. Title
 636.6′86   SF461

 ISBN 0 7028 8010 8

Printed in Great Britain by John Bartholomew and Son Limited

Contents

One: Introduction

'Softbill,' when you think about it, is an odd word. What exactly does it mean? Although it might be true up to a point it is not really meant to imply that any bird so called has a bill that crumples up like that of Donald Duck! The word, necessarily vague, is more descriptive of the food which the birds eat than of the birds themselves. I have never seen an adequate description that covers all softbills and yet remains reasonably concise. Clive Roots (1970) came near to it with "Cage and aviary birds with relatively soft bills which feed on insects including larger animal prey and soft plant material and whose young are helpless at birth," but even that is probably unnecessarily longwinded. An adequate simple working definition is "any small to medium land bird which feeds on softbodied food." Such a definition as this immediately precludes most raptors such as owls, waders, ducks, finches and parrots. Even allowing for the indistinct margins, some birds are still difficult to categorise—many crows for instance—but even so, the catchment area does not exclude any bird which should rightly be in.

This book is fortunate to have as its subject a sunburst of birds that nothing short of fantasy can improve upon. Aesthetically, they are bright, colourful, lively, somewhat romantic visions, with voices which are among the most beautiful, enchanting and evocative of all.

To aviculturists, softbills represent something else: a *challenge*. The reasons, will become apparent as the book unfolds but, in a nutshell, compared to many popular birds, softbills are, to put it mildly, usually extremely reluctant to breed freely. But it is important that we try, and try hard, if we are not soon to lose from our aviaries for ever these birds which even though they cry out for specialization, add breadth and variety to all mixed collections.

Softbilled birds are familiar to everyone even though their avicultural name may not be. Many of our common garden birds come within this category: birds such as thrushes, robins, titmice, warblers and starlings. The farther south we go (or north in the Southern Hemisphere), the more softbills we encounter, for as considerable consumers of fruit and invertebrates—which are perpetually present somewhere in the tropics—softbills can live there all the year round without the need for major migrations. Therefore it is from what Europeans mainly regard as exotic countries that most of our sumptuous imported softbills originate: the birds which constitute a large proportion of the avifauna of most zoos and bird gardens.

Some typical and well-known zoo softbills are toucans, hornbills, jays, tanagers, chats, hummingbirds, sunbirds, honeycreepers and babblers: names which conjure up visions of jungles and sun-drenched plains. Placing these alongside the more homely varieties mentioned above, we get some idea of the range of softbills and the scope of this book.

It is the challenging aspect of keeping and breeding softbills, together with their allure—birds from another world—that makes them so attractive to aviculturist and hobbyist alike. They present a challenge not only when it comes to their reproduction but very often long before that becomes even a remote possibility. Their acclimatization and diet can be problematical, and this is why beginners are usually recommended to first gain general experience with 'easier' birds, such as finches.

The ambiguous phrase 'delicate' or 'fragile softbills' is often unthinkingly used. I have myself fallen into this trap on occasions, and a trap it is because softbills intrinsically are no more or less delicate than any other wild animal. In the context of their true place in life, all animals are extremely hardy—to have survived the evolutionary process until today, they have had to be—and they only become less hardy when removed by man from their allotted niche to an artificial one. Apart from which, I have worked with enough kinds of animals from hummingbirds to elephants and giraffes to know that it is not always the seemingly frail creatures that are the most vulnerable. In fact some of the toughest little animals I know are, indeed, hummingbirds: they are difficult to match in vigour, hardiness and pugnacity. I hope no-one takes these remarks as a licence for laziness or sloppiness because that would be tragic and probably fatal; they are intended more as an exercise in reason and to prevent the experts of tomorrow being put off from keeping softbills.

Because 'softbill' is not a specific term, it is not possible to describe or illustrate a standard example as, for instance, we can with a parrot, finch or bird-of-prey. However, in many other ways, they are typical birds in a way that the Budgerigar or an owl could never be. This is probably because they draw their numbers from all four corners of the world and are not, overall, highly specialized in either diet or behaviour. Softbills include carnivores, frugivores, omnivores, insectivores and nectivores; there are terrestrial softbills, perching softbills and those which are essentially aeronauts; there are nest-weavers of all kinds, hole-nesters, mud-builders and brood-parasites; and then there are superb acrobats like the titmice and treecreepers, and others like the pittas and starlings, which owe their appeal more to a rather bumbling forthrightness than to any beguiling ethereal charm; there are softbills as tiny as the Bee Hummingbird (less than 5 cm)—the world's smallest bird, and as large as the Helmeted Hornbill (127 cm): 25 times greater.

Finally, I should perhaps explain why the observant reader will notice that little if any space has been given to the *single* pet. The reason is that with very few exceptions, they are simply not suitable. Because they have not been domesticated as have the budgie, canary, Zebra Finch and Ring-necked Parakeet, they are not only true wild birds—and as such are subject to quite sufficient pressure already without having to cope with the additional burden of a heavy demand from the pet-trade—but they also lack the years of conditioning that domestication bestows upon a species. Hard on the heels of that, however, I want to point out that there is no reason why a pair or group of birds cannot be kept, and fulfill the demands of moral aviculture at the same time as satisfying those reasonable pet-owners who are content not to so much to *own* an animal, as simply be a part of its life.

The one big anomaly in the softbill realm is the mynah (which has a title to itself in this series). It is my unshakeable belief that of all softbills, the Greater Hill Mynah in particular makes one of the least suitable pets for reasons mentioned elsewhere. I do not think that a great aptitude to mimic sounds is sufficient reason on its own to incarcerate these garrulous and nomadic birds in small solitary cages. The correct place for all mynahs outside their native homelands is in roomy communal aviaries, as, indeed, it is for any other starling.

But these provisos apart, softbills are in need of *more* interest, *more* specialization and *more* devotees, not less. And hopefully this book will in some small way help to compensate for the dearth of good practical books on softbills and balance the rows which are available on finches, budgerigars, canaries and parrots etc.

Two: Accommodation and Choosing the Right Bird

It is a nice idea, but there is really no such thing as correct accommodation. 'Correct' implies perfection and the restraint of animals by caging and aviaries has to be at best a compromise of many different factors. However sophisticated an aviary, it is still a forceful restriction of free movement and could, of course, always be more sophisticated, better designed or larger. Apart from which, it is also a question of fitting the accommodation to the birds which are going to use it. A good cage for a Budgerigar would hardly be suitable for a Macaw. Likewise with softbills, and although such an extreme might be obvious to even the most inexperienced tyro, there are a thousand shades in between—all of which are important if we wish to arrive at the best possible flight cage for our own particular birds.

What does an aviary or cage have to do? In this book the word 'aviary' will be taken to comprise both the flight-cage and roosting shed as a unit. Caging suggests solitary confinement, and as we have already seen, such housing is seldom applicable to softbills. An aviary has, first of all then, to retain its inhabitants and therefore the mesh of the wire-netting must be small enough to prevent passage. Generally speaking, this entails a diameter of about 2.5 cm; it can be larger, possibly double—4.5 cm—for medium to large softbills, while the smallest birds (e.g. hummingbirds, sunbirds, flowerpeckers and titmice) have to be contained by a gauge as small as 1.5 cm.

Notwithstanding what I have already said about aviaries suiting their particular inhabitants, it is still true that the best aviary for many standard softbills will contain a good many similarities. The side-mesh being continued below ground-level and turned outwards to deter burrowing predators and other pests; the ends of the aviary and its main perches being provided with shelter while the centre of the aviary is left exposed to benefit from the cleansing effects of the elements; and the inclusion of a compact, draughtproof and dry shed with adequate perching and connected by means of closable pop-holes to the flight-cage itself.

Sheds can be brick built or timbered with a solid roof. A thick layer of peat and sand laid on a concrete base is the ideal floor or alternatively a very thin scattering of sawdust which can be

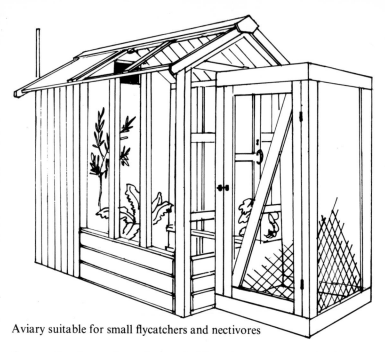

Aviary suitable for small flycatchers and nectivores

frequently changed can be used. They do not have to be large, in fact it is better if they are not; and a window should be fitted with a protection of wire-netting so that it can be left open if desired. The installation of electricity enables feeding periods to be extended on short winter days and extra heat to be provided should it become necessary. Food is best placed inside where it remains dry in wet weather and available at all times—although on long summer days there is no reason why it should not be placed outside.

Food is an obvious attraction to other animals as well as the birds for which it is intended, and should mice—usually the worst offenders—manage to penetrate your defences of wire-netting and concrete floor, it may become necessary to put down poison; this is most safely placed in a small gauge drainpipe outside the aviary and out of reach of all domestic animals and children. A simple cage-trap might also do the trick, but in the end it is better to strengthen the aviary and prevent entry in the first place. Our own interest in aviculture should not need to result in the destruction of other local wlidlife.

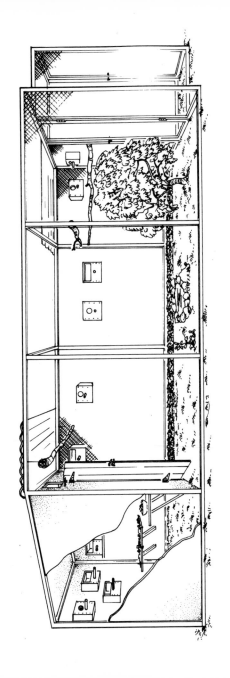

General purpose aviary

9

Aviaries should never be sited under trees where they can easily be contaminated by wild birds perching and roosting above them, and where the sun has difficulty in penetrating, so causing damp and mildew. Overhanging branches and nearby walls are also an invitation to cats, which by jumping on to the aviary at night can cause the birds to panic with fatal results if they cannot soon return to a roosting place. For this reason, a nightlight is a useful investment, failing this there should be an outside light which can be switched on in just such an emergency.

The size of an aviary is usually determined by the finance and space available: neither of which is of any consolation to the birds which have to live in it if the owner gets his priorities wrong. Space and cash are, of course, of prime importance to just about everybody but that does not mean that a small aviary need necessarily be a bad one. It all depends on how it is designed, built and landscaped *and* which birds are chosen to go into it. It is much better to build an aviary to suit the birds rather than the other way round. Apart from which, it's no good building one specially for, say, Quetzals if your chance of getting some is nil.

Hopefully, most people contemplating building a purpose-designed aviary have already done their homework and discovered by perusing dealers' lists, reading the trade and fancy journals, and talking to breeders and other enthusiasts, just what stock is available at prices they can afford. It is unusual, in my experience, for people who have reached this stage of their hobby not to have very definite ideas about the sorts of birds they want to keep.

Absolute beginners, on the other hand, will want to know the safest birds to choose—possibly to take up residence in an existing structure. I would go along with other writers who recommend that all prospective softbill fanciers should first serve their apprenticeship with the more straightforward hardbills mentioned in the Introduction before progressing on to softbills which are often more demanding in their diet if nothing else. And, of course, there is no reason why softbills should not be mixed with certain hardbills. Quite often, such 'marriages' are highly successful since the birds tend to compete less and leave each other alone more than do closely related kinds. With such differing diets, this is readily understandable. Feeding is so important in the management of softbills that it has an early chapter devoted entirely to it.

The young or aspiring softbill enthusiast must begin with one of the more versatile species, preferably an omnivore, and it is difficult to better a small corvid (crow family) which will have the accommodating habit of eating almost anything and being undemanding of sophisticated facilities. Moreover, crows and their smaller brethren—the jays—together, possibly, with the similarly named but quite separate jay- or laughing-thrushes, are usually extremely hardy, highly decorative in looks, enchanting in behaviour and voice (although too belligerent by far to be mixed with other kinds), and readily available in a wide variety of species. Aviculturally, they are rather neglected and even if one were prevented from looking after any other kind, it would be no great hardship. A collection comprised solely of these birds would not only be of great scientific value, it would also provide all the interest and challenge anyone could want.

Once experience has been gained with such fairly dependable species, the advancing enthusiast can, if desired, turn his or her attention to other sorts: maybe smaller omnivores such as thrushes, babblers and starlings (including mynah birds), and thence on to the fruiteaters, nectar-feeders and, lastly, the insectivores—probably the most difficult of all.

For most of these birds, it is not the shape of the aviary nor even its height which is most important, it is the way in which it is laid out. Where certain species do vary in their particular requirements, this will be mentioned in Chapter Six.

In respect of aviary landscaping, softbills offer far more scope than parrots, many seedeaters and birds-of-prey. Few will seriously damage growing plants and shrubs, their droppings are not nearly so caustic, and they do not strip bark nor 'chew' tender twigs and buds. A few will attack flowers—notably flowerpeckers and some sunbirds—but mostly they *use* the vegetation without destroying it: some will sip from the nectar and pollen, others will eat fruit and berries, and practically all will take advantage of the insect-life which is attracted to vegetation and cover. Indeed, this happy relationship with vegetation is one of the softbill keepers best allies: it not only does the birds inestimable psychological as well as nutritional good to feed naturally, it also takes some of the pressure off his shoulders in the summer, when providing livefood for birds feeding young is one of the most demanding tasks.

Therefore, in an ideal aviary situation, it is impossible to have too much vegetation or too many plants. Flight area is of course important but with many of the small active birds, as long as a sufficient area of shrubs are kept pruned to allow at least a metre of air-space between them and the roof, this is by far the best way of providing it. Allow some shrubs—preferably those in corners—to grow upwards because many birds deliberately seek nesting-sites as high as possible. The more vegetation there is, the more food, shelter, cover and nesting-sites there will be and the more possible territories. The main disadvantage might be that in the summer you might not see your birds quite so often; but this is the kind of sacrifice we happily make for our birds, and the one which sorts out the ego-men from the sincere, committed aviculturists—those who get their enjoyment not from pride of possession but from the knowledge that they are providing the best possible conditions and contributing something very worthwhile to zoological science in general and aviculture in particular, not to mention the lives of the birds themselves. That is what I mean when I talk of an ideal aviary situation.

The larger softbills—possibly from the Hoopoe upwards—do need more overall space with increased flying room—preferably in long uninterrupted paths—simply because they lack the manoeuvrability of the smaller kinds. But I find it hard to think of a smaller species which does not appreciate dense cover save for those like wagtails and ground-thrushes which spend much of their time at ground-level. Most small perching birds are perfectly happy to flit from bush to bush.

If ground-living birds are to be kept, then certain modifications to lay-out are necessary. Many, among them larks, pipits, buntings, ground-thrushes and wagtails, enjoy the proximity of water and rocks, and this raises another aspect of landscaping which is of great importance, for while a simple dish of water might serve the need, it lacks such a lot. A small *shallow* pool—and I stress shallow—with gently-graded sides roughened so as not to be slippery, surrounded by rockwork has much to commend it both in terms of visual appeal and direct benefit to the birds using it.

There are a few birds which do not like bathing (the above-mentioned Hoopoe is one) but to most it is an essential part of their daily lives, and there is no doubt that a good pool is immeasurably better than a possibly tiny and insecure dish with smooth and steep sides. Dishes might be simpler to provide and easier to keep clean but there is no reason why a small concrete pool should be difficult in either respect. Drainage presents no problem for water can be simply swept round and out onto the ground; ideally, it needs to be designed so that half a bucketful of water fills it to the brim. I have always found pool-cleaning, providing they are not too large and badly designed, to be easy and satisfying work, made the more so by the obvious delight shown by the birds as they swoop down to get first use of the fresh, sparkling, swirling water.

The positioning of even small concrete pools is important since once in position they generally stay put for life. If sited quite near to the entrance door, cleaning can be undertaken smoothly and without causing needless alarm to the birds. Buckets full of water and great clusters of brooms and tools are not the easiest of things to manipulate through an enclosed space. Overhanging perches—whether inside or outside the aviary—must also be avoided or removed lest the water becomes contaminated by birds' droppings. In this way the rockwork surround can be kept much cleaner.

Some birds quickly contaminate their water. Thrushes, in particular, seem to enjoy carrying food, stones, snail shells and suchlike into it—presumably for washing purposes—and aviaries housing these birds will need their water changed at least two or three times a week. Others keep it extremely clean—only using it for drinking and bathing—and their pools can go a week or more before cleaning, except in hot weather when water quickly becomes stagnant and a ready carrier of disease.

Rocks of one kind or another are necessary for certain birds to perch on if their feet are to be kept in good order; smooth rocks are easier to clean than those that have deeply pitted surfaces. Other desirable ground facilities are large logs; if part of a tree-trunk can be incorporated so much the better. Not only will it look increasingly attractive as it mellows and lichen and moss grow over it, but it will also provide the birds with an extra source of food, interest and an additional height zone for those wishing to use it.

Perching can be a thorny problem in more ways than one. It requires almost as much thought as the aviary itself and must be exactly tailored to suit those birds that are going to use it. Turacos, for instance, require only a few sturdy perches at either end of the longest flight path possible so that they can indluge in their magnificent flight which includes a gliding action, revealing their bright magenta wing-speculums. Some birds like buntings like to perch low down, but others such as tanagers prefer to be high up, while many of the smallest birds would rather have thick tangles of shrubbery through which they can creep furtively about.

As a general rule, the size of perching increases in proportion to the size of the birds, but the quantity decreases. It should always be firmly fixed so that it does not swivel or come loose—a common cause of infertility in birds since they cannot balance well enough to consummate the act. Natural branches are superior to machined dowelling because they provide a variety of diameters to exercise the birds feet properly, and their roughness keeps toe claws trimmed down. They are also cheap to replace when they become too soiled. While perches can be kept clean by scrubbing for quite a while, periodic renewal is recommended both for reasons of hygiene and the birds' mental health, since it gives them something new and fresh to explore. Birds must never be allowed to become indolent and slothful if the best is to be achieved from them. Another way of preventing boredom is by variation of diets, and this is mentioned in the next chapter.

The ground beneath the perches and elsewhere must also be considered. I am unshakeable in my belief that turf is the best possible ground cover: it is self-regenerating and to a large extent self-cleansing, moreover it is smart and does not end up looking like a prison exercise yard as concrete can so easily do. Directly beneath the perches where grass would quickly become fouled, strips of soil mixed with sand which can be hoed over each day are the simplest and most hygenic alternative to the regular scrubbing that concrete demands. If turned over every day, the soil does not sour and a healthy community of worms becomes established which quickly breaks down the organic deposits. A twice yearly spray with a weak disinfectant also helps to keep harmful bacteria at bay, although I'm afraid a severe winter is by far the best disinfectant of all.

One of the most common faults in aviary design concerns the entrance door. Under the mistaken belief that it will prevent birds from escaping, it is often made only big enough for a man to clamber through. In actual fact, the opposite is more likely to be true since you take three or four times as long to get in, quite apart from the danger of tripping yourself up with your ungainly equipment or getting wedged in the doorway! A roomy safety porch should be fitted and the door aperture must not extend to the aviary roof for when birds do escape, they invariably do it by flying along the level of the roof and over your head. If these precautions are taken, birds are unlikely to get out. Only panic normally causes such a response, and a smooth, unflustered entry

Pekin Robin

Golden fronted fruitsucker

rarely excites such; birds are usually only too happy to remain as far from you as possible. Tame birds are another matter, but even if they do escape, recapture is usually an easy matter, either by feeding into the entrance porch or in a baited trap near the aviary or on its roof.

Aviaries are best constructed out of timber (tubular metal for parrots) on top of a low stone or brick wall incorporating a damp course. The timber should be treated annually with preservative. Unfortunately, this more expensive method often has to give way to the simpler all wire-netting type. A good quality, heavy-duty wire-netting should be fixed to the *inside* of the aviary supports so as to reduce the risk of fouling caused by birds perching on the cross-members.

The shape of an aviary can be rectangular or irregular—there are points in favour of both—but square seems less satisfactory. Even more important, do not be tempted to construct a vast edifice along the lines of Lord Snowdon's aviary at London Zoo! Birds are much harder to catch (and you do occasionally have to). They are also more difficult to manage properly, and the temptation to put a large number of birds in to 'fill it up' is very strong.

Overcrowding is without doubt one of the worst crimes that the bird-keeper can commit and it is made more easier in a large aviary where you can be deceived by wide empty spaces. Many birds in captivity (and probably in the wild) like to hold the largest territory they can, and an aggressively territorial bird or pair of birds will fight weaker birds, eventually killing them, no matter how spacious the aviary is. There is much to be said for accommodating such birds (unfortunately, these include many softbills) in much smaller aviaries, perhaps in the region of $6 \times 2 \times 2.5$ m high where they can either be given sole possession or otherwise mixed with completely different kinds of birds, such as pigeons or quail.

I can recall two quite different experiences which illustrate the problems of trying to predict how birds will intermix. I once tried to introduce a pair of Violet-eared Hummingbirds into a very large, thickly-planted tropical house with a ground area of some 80 sq m; hummingbirds are predictably aggressive towards their own kind and other small birds, but I was amazed at the way in which the male ruthlessly sought out the female and tried to dispose of her. He was not content, as they often are, merely to prevent her from feeding. The other side of the coin concerns my time as a keeper at the now sadly defunct Winged World in Morecambe, Lancashire—at that time one of the best collections of softbills in the world. Because of town-council policy and public taste, as many birds as possible were put into the glass-fronted compartments, which measured in ground area only about 20 sq m on average. The resulting over-stocking altered the birds' normal behaviour patterns and very little trouble ensued. So birds which would usually have fought tooth and nail lived harmoniously together. After a while, even breeding results began to look absurdly good. As a general policy, of course, such a practice is not to be recommended, but at the Winged World it was necessary to make the best out of a bad job.

Birds, purely and simply, want enough room to move about and exercise mind and body, otherwise they, like all animals, are inherently lazy. It is a popular misconception, even among those people who should know better, that animals in captivity crave freedom above all else. But for precisely these reasons, boredom and lethargy must be guarded against, and this is best prevented by such subtle means as mentioned earlier. An obvious and potentially dire result of lethargy is obesity, and this is most likely to occur with birds in small cages or sterile, tidy aviaries, and from incorrect feeding.

Although scarcely without exception softbills do not make good cagebirds, there comes a time in the lives of nearly all aviary birds when temporary confinement in a cage is unavoidable. Maybe as a result of illness, upheaval of one sort or another in the aviary, lack of suitable permanent accommodation or during acclimatization—when cage-life is normally essential for a few weeks.

Hopefully, it is not an on-going situation, and therefore cages do not have to be ultra-sophisticated as long as they are sensibly designed. Size depends entirely on the birds in question and the reasons for their confinement. Generally, common-sense tells us if a cage is too small: the bird has to be able to hop from one perch to the other, turn around, descend comfortably to the floor and back up to the perch again. But having said that, it is also true that only rarely will a short-stay bird want to do more than that. It is a mistake to make cages too large unless they are for long-term occupation—in which case a series of box-cages like those often seen in the birdrooms of canary enthusiasts, with sliding interconnecting doors so that one long cage can be easily reduced to three or more smaller ones, and vice versa, is ideal.

Cages are like travelling-boxes, if they are too large, the birds can lose the feeling of protection gained from a confined space, and may panic and injure themselves or at best be tempted to fly round in an area which is totally unsuitable. So, accepting that a standard cage should be rectangular of regular design and appropriate size, what else should it be? First and foremost, it must be easy to clean and service, a sliding tray above a fixed base plate which prevents possible escape whilst cleaning out, is essential, as are food and water receptacles which can be attended to from *outside* the cage. One of the worst things you can do to a bird in a small cage is to thrust your hand in through the door.

One problem presented by birds confined in cages is bathing. Dishes of water on the floor or even the specially designed vessels which fit into the door aperture are either messy or not always accepted. The best alternative is mist-bathing with a fine tepid spray.

A splendid compromise between small individual cages and full outdoor aviaries are flight compartments which are usually sited indoors but can also adjoin an outside area. These are extremely useful for various purposes. Birds can convalesce in them before being thrown back into the rigours of communal aviary life, they can be utilized as useful wintering quarters for small birds which for one reason or another cannot remain outside all the year round; or provide somewhere to put other birds which might be frustrating a breeding attempt or proving dangerous to young birds, or even for a breeding pair itself; and for 'meating-off' hand-reared birds. Such a flight compartment—perhaps 2 m high and 1.5 sq m—should be available in most, if not all, collections. To provide temporary accommodation for much larger birds—either from your own collection or brought in from the wild as some most assuredly will be when the word gets round that you are a 'birdperson'—a medium-sized compartment can be invaluable and a boon when primary space reaches saturation point as it always seems to.

Once good accommodation is organised, thoughts can be turned to the exciting but serious business of actually buying and obtaining your new birds. Although they may well turn up from a variety of sources, the best bet without doubt is to obtain stock from a locally esteemed breeder. This may not be as easy as it sounds, because as we have already seen, softbills, unlike many other cagebirds, are not bred that consistently.

The most likely suppliers are dealers but great care must be exercised and whenever possible a personal visit should be undertaken so that the birds can be inspected at first hand and if liked, taken home by you. Find out as much as you can about the history of the birds in which you are most interested and ask how long they have been in the dealer's possession. Get details of the kind of diet they are used to and if wild-caught—how long since their importation and from where, and if captive-bred details of their previous owners and so on.

Choose only those birds which look lively, pert, bright-eyed, clean and in good feather. Avoid birds which are the opposite and which show signs of old age, such as heavy scaling on the legs. With flock birds, it is best to resist those which sit skulking in a corner, and the brash over-dominant ones which whizz about intimidating everyone else.

When some experience has been gained, you might be able to look at a poor specimen and believe, perhaps quite rightly, that you can save its life, bring it on, breed from it and end up with a bird or pair which does you great credit. More satisfaction is to be gained from such an enterprise than probably anything else you might undertake. But to begin with, you should err on the side of caution unless your instincts drive you strongly on.

Absolute beginners, though, are strongly recommended to enlist the aid of an older hand; and it is for reasons of contact that you should consider joining a local bird club and national society as well as visiting good collections regularly so that birds can be seen in all seasons, and at various shows, where tip-top softbills are exhibited and at which other enthusiasts might be met and befriended.

Three: Feeding

Fruit and invertebrates are the major softbill foods, and while the fruit a bird may get in the wild is easy enough (if inexpensive) to match or substitute in a foreign land, natural animal food is quite another matter. Substitutes—most notably maggots and mealworms—can be procured or bred by the aviculturist and an infinite variety collected from the wild in the summer when it is most in demand for nestlings, but with very few exceptions the diets of invertebrate feeders have to be supplemented in some other way.

Softfood is a name given by finch breeders to certain rearing foods but it is equally applicable to the mixtures concocted to please, satisfy and maintain to a healthy old age very many softbills. It can be, and usually is, made up in a wide variety of ways, using some very different ingredients. Such insectivorous foods or 'insectile-mixes', as they are often called, are universally accepted and unlikely ever to be supplanted.

A tried, tested and proven home-made recipe is set out below; I first encountered it while working at the Winged World, and have since introduced it elsewhere most successfully. The ingredients vary in their availability from area to area but it is generally possible to approximate them quite closely. It is a complete food, containing all the necessary vitamins, protein, carbohydrates and trace elements. In the interests of variety, fail-safety and experimentation, this mixture can be altered from time to time without losing site of the original. Other tit-bits or 'interest-foods' should continue to be offered whenever possible. It is reassuring that birds living contentedly on an insectile-mix are not prey to transport, dock or other strikes nor the seasonability and perishability of sweet fruit and insects. Softfood is not messy, fiddly or time-consuming to prepare, and it has a wholesomeness that is pleasant and satisfying.

There is very little wastage because it is easy to gauge the amount to give to each aviary by what is left from the previous feed; moreover, because of its semi-moist consistency, birds are obliged to consume elements that are beneficial to them but which they would perhaps be unwilling or unable to take if presented in another way. I doubt if there is a softbill—excepting nectivores—in the world that would not benefit from such a food. Even specialist fruit-eaters such as turacos and toucans achieve a much-needed breadth of diet when this mixture is sprinkled on top of their prepared fruit and mixed in so that it adheres.

The basic dry mixture keeps for a long time and can be finally prepared to a crumbly consistency by using molten honey or invert sugar together with water as the wetting agents in weekly or fortnightly batches. It is thus constantly available at a moment's notice. For just one or two pet birds, commercially prepared equivalents are readily obtainable and probably the best option, but for all medium to large collections the commercial foods are more expensive and rather less satisfying to the serious aviculturist and possibly the birds themselves. Sometimes proprietary softfoods go sour if kept too long or are incorrectly stored. Home-made mixes can be made up in smaller quantities so that freshness is assured and the ingredients and proportions known exactly: quality control in fact. Storage should be in a dark, cool and dry place and in some kind of impervious container such as a plastic bread bin, galvanised silo or polythene sack.

A base of fine softfood makes an ideal vehicle for offering livefood such as maggots and mealworms to birds. In a steep-sided dish, they remain in good condition until needed by the birds. Furthermore, the birds cannot help but get some of the softfood even if they do not want it and end up with two meals in one. For every single insectivorous bird one drop of concentrated vitamins A, D and E should be added to the maggots each morning. Foraging also provides the birds with a useful mental exercise and prevents them from consuming all the choicest items literally in one fell swoop. The insects remain in better condition because they escape desiccation in hot sunshine; all the same, livefood should always be fed in two stages—early morning and mid-afternoon (early evening in the summer).

Mention of livefood inevitably raises the questions of cost, availability, suitability and home-production. Unless you are exceptionally talented, lucky or have unlimited time at your disposal, it is unlikely that you will ever be able to breed enough live insects to sustain indefinitely even one bird. But what you can do, is breed enough to supplement their normal diet and possibly from time to time give them a special treat in place of the regular meal. Subtle variation of diet is a most beneficial way of sustaining a bird's interest in life and staving off lethargy—which is a real killer. Also, livefood is just about the best thing that you can offer all sorts of different nestlings.

However anti-social an activity it might be, maggots are easy enough to produce in the summer. If red meat or offal is suspended beneath a rudimentary shelter, it soon becomes covered with the eggs of flies which, in turn, quickly develop into maggots. A tray of bran placed underneath the meat will catch and hold the full-grown maggots as they drop off the meat to pupate. It is wise to site such a 'maggot factory' away from dwellings and leeward of the prevailing wind.

Breeding mealworms is much safer but less predictable. There are many different systems: most are variations on the following basic theme. A large rectangular container—often called a 'coffin'—and made of wood is three-quarters filled with bran and layers of crumpled newspaper, brown paper or woollen material. To provide moisture, a few fresh banana skins can be laid on top and replaced every few days or a dampened sponge can be used. Mealworms are introduced and allowed to feed, pupate, metamorphase into little meal-beetles, grow, lay eggs and finally hatch into a new generation of mealworms which, once sufficiently grown, can be fed to the birds. Young mealworms are especially valuable for the smaller birds. It is important to set aside some young adults to breed the next generation. Rearing mealworms is quite a complicated business, and it becomes more so if you take it a stage further and try to establish a rotation of smaller self-contained units which should, theoretically, provide a more constant supply.

There are other sorts of livefood which the enthusiast can endeavour to breed but none so widespread or useful. Crickets and locusts are two of the best, and I have had more success breeding locusts than any other insect even though, on the face of it, their requirements seem more demanding. What is more, they are very interesting in themselves. A suitable locust breeding cage is illustrated. Some of the most important points to remember are to provide *continual* heat (it is doubtful if you will ever get it too hot), food in the form of fresh grass and deep sand containers in which the females can lay their eggs. The sand should be sprayed lightly to maintain a certain amount of humidity. A glass front is also convenient so that you can see what is happening without frightening them. The 'hoppers' on hatching are very tiny and although they grow fast, they are capable of escaping through the slightest of cracks and therefore any breeding cage must be extremely well constructed. Locusts of all ages are suitable for a wide variety of different sized birds.

A. Heat source

B. Deep sand tray for eggs

C. Fresh grass

D. Thermometer

E. Ventilation holes covered by gauze

Glass-fronted locust-breeding cage

Stick-insects are another occasional bird food and sometimes appear as such in advertisements in the technical press. I feel that such interesting animals are better kept for their own sake and that the commoner and cheaper maggots and mealworms are usually quite sufficient. Both are obtainable from commercial breeders—maggots are, of course, bred in large numbers as fishing bait and can be bought in bulk direct from breeders or in smaller quantities (they are sold by the pint) from angling shops.

Mealworms are only widely obtainable by post from specialist avicultural, food or pet suppliers; they can be kept in good condition and for long periods in a simple bran container as described above. Maggots, on the other hand, quickly pupate if not kept in a refrigerator and while they remain a good food—appreciated by some birds—they are no longer universally popular. Maggots intended as food for birds should not be fed themselves since botulism can be passed to the birds in this way. Indeed, it is prudent to always keep maggots for a week or so, changing their meal-bath at least twice before using them. The maggots ingest the meal thereby cleaning the gut. I have found grass meal to be by far the best cleansing agent since it is very finely ground and contains many advantageous properties which the birds thus obtain via the maggots. It is, you will note, a main ingredient in our insectile mix.

One kind of livefood that I have not yet mentioned in detail is the wild sort, and this can often come to the rescue in the summer when young birds are making heavy demands. I naturally recoil from going out into the countryside, thrashing about with a net and terrorising the local insect population but the need does sometimes arise. When it does, the best way of collecting a wide selection of insects is to sweep gently and methodically through long grass with a wide rimmed net. An ants' nest full of cocoons (commonly miscalled 'ants-eggs') can provide a bountiful feast while larger insects and spiders (invaluable for sunbirds) can be hunted individually for specific purposes.

If livefood demands time, trouble and expense, fruit is at least easier to store and obtain though it is getting increasingly expensive. And this highlights one of the main arguments against keeping softbills: expense. They are undoubtedly more expensive to keep than hardbills; for one reason, the perishable nature of their food means that it has to be frequently bought in small quantities, while seed can be purchased in bulk when supplies are at their cheapest and stored almost indefinitely.

Sweet apples, pears and other hard fruits are the cheapest and least perishable, and they form an adequate base for most frugivores' diets, but it is the softer fruits—bananas, grapes, tomatoes, melon, sultanas and raisins—which cannot be ignored and yet which are extremely expensive. They throw the keeper into a dilemma: how little to spend while still giving his birds a sufficiently varied diet? Just because, for instance, your birds love grapes and appear to sulk if denied them, it does not *necessarily* mean that they are essential to them.

Fruit should be diced—using a very fine sharp knife. Cut the pieces rather smaller than might seem necessary, because although it cannot be too small, if it is too large, there is a risk of the bird choking. It is better to leave the fruit whole or simply halved to be pecked at, than fail to cut it small enough. Once diced and the correct amount of each kind placed in the appropriate dish, it is quite a good idea to mix it up with the softfood—in this way, either the least popular sorts are consumed along with the favourite items or are made more palatable by the juices of, for example, tomato, orange and grapes.

With a little practice and generally a few sliced fingers, it is possible to become extremely skilled at cutting up fruit. There are several shortcuts and each fruit has, in my experience, to be tackled from a different angle, but there is fun in discovering these for yourself. Fruits like bananas and oranges have to be peeled (although the latter can be just cut into halves or quarters and spiked on a twig) but there is no need to do so with apples, pears, grapes and tomatoes.

Because we are not all dieticians and nutritionists—and even if we were and knew the correct values of different foods—it is not feasible to arrive exactly at the cheapest and yet best diet for each individual bird. For safety's sake, we verge on the generous side and perhaps give our birds more of what they like and extra delicacies—they do depend on us totally after all—and most of us probably spend rather more than we absolutely need to.

Since fruit is so expensive and fruiterers cannot or will not sell blemished wares, it is a good idea to befriend your local greengrocer or fruiterer. He might often be able to let you have a damaged or partly bad box for next to nothing. It is surprising the amount of sound fruit you can salvage from an apparently ruined case but do *not* be tempted to offer your birds anything you would not yourself eat, and do not on any account feed over-ripe grapes, bananas, pears or melon.

Apples and pears contain much goodness but are not liked so much as the less beneficial banana and are usually left until last; but it is important to make the birds finish all suitable food before being given more of what they like most. Oranges work as a laxative on softbills and although appreciated should only be given in small quantities. Grapes are enjoyed by all softbills, and are the equivalent of mealworms for insectivores although far less substantial. Few can resist them and they are enjoyed by many different sorts of birds—not just softbills.

If steeped in hot water and left to soak overnight so that they swell, soften and are digestible, raisins and sultanas are another invaluable food. Most birds like a few each day and even the water need not be wasted since it adds flavour and goodness to the insectile-mix if added to it as part of the final mixing process.

Incidentally, if maggots are offered to insectivores in such a base as recommended, it should not be too wet or the maggots will gain traction up the sides of the dish and escape.

Softbills should be fed ad lib—they cannot as a rule endure prolonged periods between meals because either the high water content of their food means rapid digestion or the food itself is proportionately less nutritious. And so anyone considering keeping softbills should reckon on at least two feeds per day. Even if the second feed is not necessary, it is asking for trouble not to check that enough food remains to last until the next morning. Nectar-feeders certainly require two separate feeds every day especially during hot weather when their mixes can quickly sour. Pairs of birds and even groups tend to consume approximately the same amount of food every day, and this eventually enables you to gauge precisely the quantities to set before them each morning. The laudable desire to cut down on wastage means that you naturally endeavour to have as little uneaten food as possible remaining next morning, and this may tempt you to pare away your safety margin. Two or three times a year, the birds will, without warning increase their intake significantly; an increase of energy expenditure due to

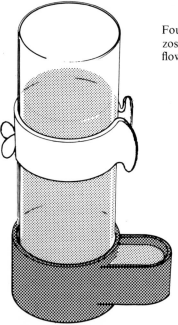

Fountain for sunbirds, spider hunters, zosterops, honey-creepers and flowerpeckers

pre-breeding activity, moulting or colder weather will increase the birds' food requirements. It is impossible to predict *exactly* when this will occur, so if no evening check is made, distressed, weakened and even dead birds can result. I have frequently been surprised on finding a dish picked spotlessly clean by late afternoon when a half or third full one was expected. Another point to remember is that if a softbill has been going hungry, it will take an inordinate length of time to get back to normal eating. Observation and diligence are therefore necessary at all times.

Besides insectivores and frugivores, the other main categories of softbilled birds are nectar-feeders and omnivores. The latter by definition are the easiest to feed since they make the most of whatever is going (although they still need a balanced diet) but nectivores are quite different. It is not that they are difficult to feed—surprisingly, quite the reverse—it is more a question of what to feed. There is plenty of academic controversy about the best food for hummingbirds, sunbirds and others less specialised such as white-eyes (zosterops), flowerpeckers and spiderhunters.

It is not an argument to get embroiled in here, so all I will say is that along with many other professional birdkeepers I place my complete faith in an American high protein invalid food called Super Hydramin. Hummingbirds fed on this have bred at San Diego Zoo in California and elsewhere. It is common practice with nectar-feeders to give them a high protein feed first thing in the morning before the day's activity, following it in the evening before they go to roost with a weaker solution of simple sugar and water.

During short winter days, the photoperiod (hours of light) should be artificially extended enabling the smaller species—especially the nectivores—to have a more natural feeding period. It is asking too much of a hummingbird, sunbird or flycatcher to go 14 or 15 hours without food on a regular basis, and a feeding extension of five or six hours is wise management.

Nectar-feeders generally have a very high metabolism and burn up their food quickly. Theoretically, the strength of artificial nectar is not of too much importance: the stronger it is, the less frequently birds will feed and vice versa. However, the digestive processes of nectivorous birds is designed to accept and digest food rapidly, and the birds should therefore be encouraged to visit the nectar tubes regularly—every ten minutes or so when active. In effect, a compromise is struck between neat water and pure protein; with experience soon determining the correct strengths and amounts.

It is important to provide a further feeding station for each additional nectivore in the aviary to prevent one dominant bird from taking up a territory near a feeding tube and preventing all others from visiting it. There are different styles of feeding devices for each group of nectar-feeders.

Feeding tube for hummingbirds

Hummingbirds feed on the wing, hovering in front of a special tube suspended in mid-air; sunbirds, honeycreepers and white-eyes are less able flyers and prefer to perch and feed from a tube with a wider aperture at its base; larger varieties are content to take their food at ground level either from an inverted jam-jar dispenser or merely from an open dish—although this way the food gets fouled more quickly.

I have left until now mention of one form of livefood because it is more relevant to nectar-feeders than anything else. Drosophilae, more commonly known as fruit-flies, are small brown-bodied flies which soon appear if over-ripe bananas etc. are left about in warm weather. A culture can easily be established by putting old soft fruit in large deep tins and maintained even through the winter in a warm room if a constant supply of old food is regularly provided for the females to lay their eggs on. At a temperature of no more than 24°C, the breeding cycle takes only seven days, but any hotter and the success rate drops. The easiest way to offer the mature insects to birds is to put a top on one of the tins, placing it in the cage with the lid just ajar so that the insects can creep out one by one, whereupon they will be eagerly snapped up by the birds which quickly come to recognise the sight of their picnic hamper, and you approaching with it. I believe that quite apart from the nutritional benefits of this superb natural food to the birds, the mental diversion provided by the actual hunting of the insects cannot be overemphasized.

Constant experimentation, observation and resourcefulness are the three main prerequisites of the amateur softbill dietician. Much more than with most other birds is there a need to keep an open mind. All sorts of different and new foods can be offered—the worst thing that can happen is that it will be ignored.

The birds least likely to ignore food are, of course, the omnivores. Whether they lean towards animal or vegetable food, they are highly obliging in their habitual willingness to accept all sorts of food from table-scraps (if wholesome and not given to excess) to the very best fruit etc. Using fruit and a coarse insectile-mix as a nucleus omnivores can be given lean raw meat, roughage in the form of small animals, a little of the more expensive fruit plus a small amount of livefood, although this is seldom essential and if supplies are short, it should be the first item to be omitted.

Peanuts and other nuts are much appreciated by some, especially jays and magpies, and many enjoy the therapeutic exercise of opening up peanuts and hazelnuts for themselves although they can seldom manage anything tougher. These birds and their brethren will occasionally catch the odd snail, mouse or worm if the aviary is well planted; 'natural' features such as dry stone walls are also a big help. Cheese is enjoyed by most omnivores, and dried cheese is probably even better than fresh since it has had most of the oil extracted.

A few softbills have more specialized carnivorous tendencies than the catholic omnivores and, in fact, any bird which feeds to a large extent on small vertebrates, invertebrates and large insects should be regarded for avicultural purposes as a carnivore. Typical of these are shrikes and some kingfishers, notably the Kookaburra. Small strips of lean red meat, the length of a matchstick and two or three times as broad, in a dish of shallow water are accepted with alacrity by a great many softbills, and if not fed to excess make an ideal food. To the carnivores they form a staple diet.

With some species, especially nectivores like the Scarlet-chested Sunbird and the minivets, colourfoods—some of which contain synthetic canthaxanthin—are often added to the standard diet to help them remain in good colour. I have found that with a bird as colourful as a flamingo, the grass meal already mentioned in this chapter contains enough of the essential carotenoid organic compound to keep it in fairly *true* colour. Likewise, Scarlet Ibis have been kept in good colour on a diet of nothing other than day-old chicks. The exaggerated crimson-ness brought about by some of the artificial colour-foods is as inappropriate as the washed out appearance of other specimens; although grassmeal cannot, of course, be given to sunbirds very easily!

Grit is an important item in the lives of hardbills and all those birds needing to grind food in the crop—it is therefore of very little importance to softbills, and if they need it at all, they can generally obtain all they need from the ground and the mortar of walls. If kept in cages, insectivores and carnivores in particular should be allowed access to some fine grit.

Four: General Management

Correct management of birds begins from the moment you get them home—if not before—and that means acclimatization; not necessarily the major acclimatization that newly imported animals are subjected to (which, these days, usually means quarantine as well) but a secondary form. This is just as important and involves a bird settling in to both a new environment when bought as a young *or* old specimen, and a new owner. For no matter how closely you endeavour to match the previous diet and housing, it can never be done absolutely; even the very act of catching and transportation involves considerable stress and upheaval.

There is a third minor category of acclimatization when a bird is simply moved from one cage or aviary to another, and this will be mentioned later. It is secondary acclimatization which is of most concern to us. Before any bird is ordered let alone acquired, its long-term accommodation and management plan should already have been decided upon. On arrival, it is wise to place the birds in smallish cages where they can be observed closely and attended to individually.

Some keepers believe in administering antibiotics to all new arrivals under the belief that they will then start off with a clean sheet. Indeed they will since most bacteria will have been destroyed—harmful and beneficial alike—and the birds will not only have been cleared of many potential killers but also, unfortunately, the means of fighting off many more which the stress of upheaval can so easily trigger off, and so the prudent keeper tends to administer a broad-spectrum antibiotic only when a bird shows definite signs of illness.

During the acclimatization process, the birds are gradually weaned on to their new diet and get the chance to become adjusted to a new owner. This period need only last a few days; a little experience soon tells the aware keeper when a bird is ready to move on to its future home and when any further delay is likely to be counter-productive.

Correct diets for softbills have already been discussed but there is no harm in giving a new arrival a lot of what it likes in order to win its confidence. There will be plenty of time later for establishing a more properly balanced diet. You cannot and must not attempt to discipline wild animals—to do so is the hallmark of a pet-owner, not an avilculturist.

All birds but particularly newcomers like to feel the security of a routine, for in captivity the owner takes on the role of Mother Nature and is relied upon to provide all. A routine helps to set up this underlying confidence which supports the whole fabric of captive management. The alleviation of boredom, important if breeding results are to be the best possible, has to be achieved within the confines of this routine and not by chopping and changing it.

Primary acclimatization is not the subject for this book since it is now undertaken only by professionals—either dealers or experienced importers. Import and export restrictions around the world have quite rightly been strengthened and casual or one-off importations are now virtually a thing of the past. All animals entering Britain are subject to quarantine under Government regulations. This means that newly imported birds acquired by private individuals will already have been through one strenuous period of acclimatization, and it will pay the new owner to find out exactly how the birds have been looked after, for how long and on what they have been fed, and to approximate this as closely as possible.

It is probably as well, as soon as you think the birds have got over their move and are feeding well, not to delay placing them in their permanent home any longer. If there is no alternative but to put them in with existing residents (and this is always a dangerous operation seldom without repercussions) the correct time of the day to do so is noon. By then, they will have at least one good feed and have the afternoon and evening ahead of them in which to find a roosting place for the night. To be introduced at any other time is asking for trouble. It is also an operation to be carried out only in settled weather, and this tends to rule out the movement of birds in winter. Late summer is the best time: the territorial activities and passions of breeding are waning, young birds are about and older ones are hopefully more concerned with fattening up for the winter.

But do not be misled, you can still have serious problems and it is always better to introduce new birds into an empty aviary even if it means removing the residents for a few days until the newcomers have settled in. Experience is the only real guide but the amount of time allowed to lapse before replacing the original birds is crucial: it depends more on the individual than the species. It could be anything from one day to a couple of weeks. Leave it too long

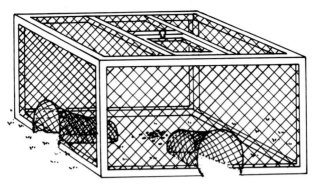

Wire cage trap with funnel entrances

though and the new birds may themselves become too territorial and reject the old ones! An extra dish of food in a different place is a wise precaution.

One of the fundamental management jobs is, of course, cleaning—softbills are particularly messy in this respect and do need regular attention. Certainly aviaries should be attended to every other day and possibly even more frequently than that except during a delicate breeding attempt, although when a routine has been established, it is surprising what most nesting birds will tolerate. It is now almost a recognised part of breeding raptors to leave them strictly alone just before and during the breeding season, but this practice is neither practicable or necessary with softbills.

By cleaning I do not mean strenuous scrubbing but such tasks as hoeing the earth beneath the perches. A certain amount of scrubbing does have to be done but if the daily routine is undertaken diligently, major cleaning is only infrequently needed: little and often is the best plan. Perches need scrubbing and replacing occasionally but a lot depends on their siting and the kinds of birds using them.

Inside sheds are rather a different matter since the floor is not in the least self-cleansing and the weather cannot help you. Therefore, if it is used for roosting or feeding it is necessary to clean the floor once a week, but a scanty layer of sawdust is all that is needed.

Small cages and indoor flight cages need daily attention if they are to remain in good condition and hygienic. And they are in most ways more of a problem than outdoor aviaries. A major headache is the stress unavoidably caused birds by working extremely close to them; in an aviary you will generally find that the inmates sit quietly at the opposite end to that which you are working at.

The imposition of stress is one of the few arguments against mist-bathing birds in cages, and if a bird really does hate it and shows no signs of coming round, then it is probably as well to substitute a dish of water. Many birds enjoy the experience though and others grow to. It really is the only way of allowing hummingbirds to bathe since they never use standing water. Many other small softbills are either rain-bathers or leaf-bathers and they too generally prefer mist-spraying. Outside it is seldom if ever necessary.

The general impression the reader will have got by now of the unsuitability of softbills to cage life is confirmed by their relative scarcity in organised cagebird shows—which are much more suited to finches and parrots. Some people do keep softbills for showing and will strongly defend their interest. However, such a softbill is unlikely to breed while it is in show condition because of the impositions and disciplines of the showing syndrome: the very time of a birds life, it should be remembered, that it is also in prime breeding condition. The practice of buying in birds just for shows has no place in pure aviculture which, literally defined, means the culture or breeding of birds.

It says much for the initial impact of softbills that they often win the Best in Show prize, even if, in my experience, the winner is not always the 'best', only the most striking or unusual. Undoubtedly the bird has to be in good condition but so far as a 'standard' goes, there is often simply nothing to compare it with—a very different state of affairs from showing budgerigars or canaries.

However the softbill sections are always some of the most interesting parts of the show because you never quite know just what you will find there. It is indicative of today's import and export regulations that the softbill entries in shows are declining. It really is one branch of aviculture in dire need of a serious and sustained captive-breeding effort. My experiences do not instill me with optimism for the avicultural future of softbills; there are too many one-off breedings and not enough emphasis put on propagation to second, third and subsequent generations.

The idea of uprooting a bird from an aviary where it has settled down to shove it into a travelling box, send it all around the country and thence into a show cage where it is jostled and peered at from close quarters seems to me a sublime form of torture which we should not impose on any bird which is not absolutely conditioned to it—and there are not many softbills accustomed to that as a breed. I know that showbird people point out that only 'trained' birds are entered in shows, but the very fact that training is necessary at all in some ways says enough. In the end, it all depends on whether you are keeping birds to boost your own ego or whether you genuinely and sincerely want to study and breed them for their own sake.

Movement of birds raises the question of how to actually catch them. The very worst thing you can do is chase the wretched creature about the aviary, ineffectually waving a net at it until it succumbs in a corner through sheer terror and exhaustion. There is certainly a knack to catching birds with a net, and I'm not so sure that it can be learned from experience. I have known plenty of experienced keepers who are more likely to brain a bird than catch it.

In any medium to large aviary, it is far better to devise some form of trap unless the birds can be restricted to a shed. The best traps are those which lure a bird in through a funnel by food and retain it because of the bird's inability to find the opening again owing to its position near the centre of the cage and not around the side. The spring trap in which a trapdoor is triggered by a bird alighting on a sprung perch is another good method, but I prefer the former because in a mixed aviary there is more chance of capturing the desired bird at the first attempt, thereby reducing the stress imposed on all the other birds as well. Where there is just a single pair of birds, the second sort works just as quickly and efficiently.

When a bird is moved, sold or exchanged, especially in a large collection, it is important to record the fact in such a way that it can be referred back to whenever necessary. This is certainly true if a serious breeding programme is envisaged. Records obviously call for the positive identification of individuals, and this generally means ringing or banding. Close-ringing of nestlings as done by breeders of birds-of-prey and cagebirds for legal reasons is not recommended for nervous softbills; disturbance of birds at such a critical time is courting disaster in the most foolhardy way. Ideally, the correct time to ring softbills and, for that matter, most wild caged birds (i.e. those not conditioned to virtual domestication) is on their removal from the parent aviary or before being put into a new one—which is also the correct time to ring new arrivals—so that they are caught up and handled as little as possible.

Rings

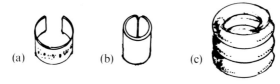

(a)   (b)   (c)

(a) Metal. Fitted with special pliers
(b) Plastic split ring. Fitted with special tool which prises open ring over tarsus
(c) Chicken-type ring which furls over the legs of larger birds

It is a different type of ring to that used for close-ringing which, as the name implies, refers to an unbroken band designed to slip over the foot of a young nestling and on to the tarsus where it remains for life unable to return over the foot or slip over the ankle (knee) because these will soon have grown to render this impossible. Split-rings are usually plastic—either the chicken type which is furled over the leg or a stiffer simpler ring which is prised open and placed on the leg by a special tool—or a metal one which is simply closed around the tarsus with special pliers. Rings are numbered or coded so that a bird once rung is permanently identifiable.

For most softbills—that is all except the large and extremely small—the best way of holding them is with the head protruding from between the first and second fingers which gently but firmly grip the neck, and the body nestling in the hand with its back to the palm; the thumb and third finger together with the other hand are then free to do most manipulatory tasks. Very small birds such as hummingbirds are completely concealed by the hand and have to be handled very carefully, while larger birds above, say, the size of a small hornbill usually need two people. It is a bird like medium-sized thrush which is most easily handled, although its frailty when compared with our strength must never be forgotten. It seems very likely that the attitude of the person involved together with his or her sensitivity and flair affect the birds' confidence, and it is very noticeable that while a bird will lie peacefully in one person's hand, it will struggle violently in another's. Again as with catching-up, it is possibly an inherent 'skill' and not easily learned.

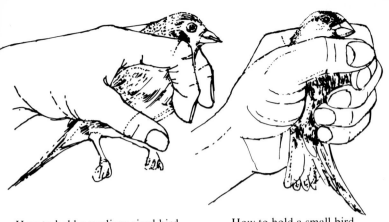

How to hold a medium-sized bird 　　How to hold a small bird

A card index system or something similar which contains full details of each bird's history and its subsequent health and development together with all breeding attempts and their results becomes an invaluable reference library. Such a system will prove its worth over and over again, and is a mine of information when plans are formulated, reports written and birds sold.

As we have already seen, one of the biggest management problems crops up when it becomes necessary to mix birds, whether they are of different or similar species, and unfortunately only through experience formed out of trial and error and possibly intuition can we begin to understand the problem. There are however several guidelines to bear in mind along the way, and many of these are mentioned in the chapter which deals with the peculiarities of particular species and types but it is even more a problem of the individual. Even true pairs are sometimes prone to disagreements which can quickly escalate into serious, sometimes fatal, conflicts; any experienced keeper will be able to recount one instance after another. All you can generally do on such occasions is remove the aggressor (assuming its victim is not badly injured) and reintroduce it a day or two later. Such stormy relationships are, I'm afraid, in the nature of many softbills, and there is little to be done about it. I have had these distressing experiences with all sorts of birds from hummingbirds to toucans and some of the worst offenders were beautifully coloured, medium-sized birds such as leafbirds and rollers.

The more carnivorous birds like starlings, jay-thrushes and corvids are more predictably dangerous, and it is unwise to mix such birds save with utterly different kinds—preferably not softbilled at all. Tempting as it is to regard all such awkwardness as a nuisance, we must remember that it is us who have confined the birds in unnatural surroundings; we can hardly expect them to cope with such an upheaval any better than we would. In the case of the rollers, for instance, pairs only meet up naturally for breeding, spending the rest of the year separately; moreover, they are habitually intolerant of similarly-sized birds, and conditioned to spending their days in the boundless skies.

Five: Breeding

For softbills to breed successfully they require contentment, routine, peace and quiet and a compatability of sexes. Luck too plays a major part: without it, you can flounder hopelessly for years no matter how painstakingly you can make your preparations; but, conversely, with luck on your side, even the least promising situations can turn out to be unbelievably fertile. To a large extent, luck decides the character of the birds you buy and even their sexes if this is not visually apparent; therefore it tends to decree their compatability.

You have to hope you are lucky and carry on doing your best. With most domestic and pet animals, breeding is a foregone conclusion, if anything they usually prove too prolific, but softbilled birds practically without exception are quite the opposite. We should never forget that we are dealing with *wild* animals, and inducing them to breed occupies the minds of many dedicated and experienced aviculturists and scientists. That is not to say that the private individual cannot achieve remarkable success—indeed, many of the major breakthroughs to date in softbill breeding owe thanks to their efforts.

Once we have chosen our birds, given them the best possible accommodation, devised the correct diet, and established a routine to their liking, we can turn our minds to encouraging their propagation instead of just hoping for the best. The first thing to consider—assuming the aviary has already been suitably planted— is a nesting device of one sort or another, preferably a selection. This can take the form of a conventional nestbox or a flat platform, it depends entirely on the species involved. Chapter 7 should help in this respect but it will pay any aspiring breeder to read up as much as he can about his birds in the wild and approximate their natural preferences as closely as possible.

It is yet another argument for imagination and resourcefulness. There is much you can do to encourage a reluctant pair to breed: a selection of nesting sites, a wide variety of materials with which to build, a corner of the aviary left strictly alone, a diet sufficient in every respect, a living-space designed to stimulate the mind and body, screening from extraneous sounds and activities, the correct aviary companions or none at all and a positive attitude emanating from yourself which may well rub-off on your birds.

Some birds—barbets immediately come to mind—like to

excavate their own nesting and roosting chambers. An upright old log or tree trunk is appreciated not only by barbets but by many other softbills, while prostrate logs are used by all manner of ground-loving birds—among them pittas, thrushes and wagtails.

Other birds including some sunbirds and flycatchers like to nest above running water and there is no reason why the enterprising breeder should not construct an environment conducive even to those birds with a need such as this.

One of the most successful ruses for encouraging softbills to breed is to begin building their nests for them. This will often trigger the appropriate response, and from the clumsy, haphazard foundations formed by human inexpert fingers, the birds will take over and finish the job or begin one of their own in a site chosen by themselves. I have found this method particularly successful with corvids, thrushes and doves (some of which, of course, are softbilled). It could be argued that to erect a nestbox achieves exactly the same object, but that is a traditional ploy of the ornithologist brought into the avicultural sphere and by now well known and used.

Nestboxes are certainly of tremendous value to aviculturists, although of less importance with softbills than with seedeaters because many are simply not hole-nesters. Many medium-sized softbills build the conventional cup-shaped nest with which we are all familiar. The open-fronted box is of more use for certain species than the usual style with a small entrance hole, as used by tits and nuthatches. But it is a good idea to provide a wide selection at different heights and with different aspects if it is not known exactly what is required. Nestboxes should face away from the prevailing wind and be sheltered from direct sunshine and torrential rain.

Open-fronted nestbox

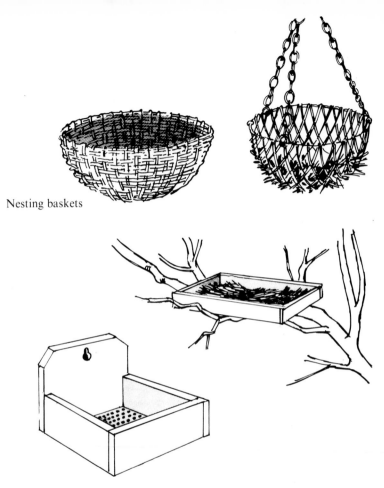

Nesting baskets

Nestboxes used by many large softbills

There are those birds that like to nest high up (including some tanagers) and those which will only nest near ground level like the pittas, and although it is again advisable to make a study of the birds' natural habits, and plant or design the aviary accordingly, it is probably best for all aviaries to possess some dense cover at all levels and preferably be undisturbed there as well. Wire-trays of one sort or another can be secured amongst the foliage to provide a base for such birds as need them.

Birds cannot build nests unless they have suitable material, and it is surprising how often this is overlooked. Most in fact require a succession of different materials beginning with stout twigs, progressing on to thinner twigs and ending up with rootlets, grasses and moss; some species have to be given mud. Certain of the smallest birds use cobwebs but these are difficult to collect.

Ever since I lost a brood of turacos from aspergillosis contracted from the straw that I supplied as nesting material, I have been afraid of such substances unless cultured first. Fortunately there are suitable substitutes, and I have found the packaging material known as 'wood-straw' a good one providing it is cut into reasonably short lengths so that its extreme strength cannot strangle or otherwise harm the birds. A similar but more finely shredded straw is also sometimes available which is even better.

Again and again the question of resourcefulness arises: with regard to nesting material, the best use has to be made of whatever is to hand or can be found. Animal fur, dog-combings for example, is an obvious natural material which is ideal for putting the finishing touches to otherwise completed nests.

Birds are very secretive when it comes to nesting—the rollers are a good case in point—and if such activity is suspected, it is important not to investigate to find out what is going on. Be sure to resist the urge to investigate, and the same goes if you know or believe there to be youngsters. The adults behaviour will give them away if you watch closely enough and you will be able to provide the extras they need without actually having to confirm the event visually.

The temptation to have 'just a peek' is great and you will think of many justifications to do so, all of which must be firmly disregarded. Records and curiosity are both less important than the lives of the youngsters. While it is true that incubation is a hazardous time, it is easy to think that once it has been successfully accomplished, the rest is downhill—unfortunately this is not so. The actual rearing is pervaded with a terrifying assortment of pitfalls and problems. Undoubtedly, disturbance and stress must take some, if not much, of the blame. Coupled to this must be diet and, probably of unappreciated importance, an incorrect psychological state.

Fostering eggs out to more reliable parents which is so often the salvation of finches and other seedeaters, is seldom practicable with softbills: nor is the use of incubators because of the difficulty of hand-rearing.

Assuming that some eggs have hatched, the business of providing the parent(s) with all it or they need begins. Very often the male has to be removed in case he proves dangerous to the mother or her babies. As it is not always possible to know when or if this is likely to occur, many aviculturists remove them as a matter of course after the eggs have been laid, and this is probably wise with many birds including those as dissimilar as magpies and sunbirds. With others though it is one of the worst things you can do: both sexes of starlings rear the young, and hornbills of course are an even better example. More often than not it is a question of the individual, and it is not always possible to be specific.

If the male of a brooding female shows any signs of annoying her he should be removed. The chances are that he will only be a danger and a nuisance throughout the operation but until such time as he does blot his copybook, it is best to give him the benefit of the doubt. Try not to upset the equilibrium of the aviary and the female when catching the male—it is far better to use a trap than a net.

Irrespective of whether or not the male is removed, the same care and attention to detail has to be exercised in and around the breeding environs. The food intake will steadily increase and this must be anticipated; it must, moreover, be the right sort of food, in the right proportions and with a suitable variety of extras. This sounds a tall order but it is not nearly as bad as it seems. The parents' normal diet is still provided in the same way but supplemented accordingly. Livefood is increased if the birds are insectivorous or omnivorous. Even some frugivores will take livefood and nectivores invariably rear their young exclusively on live insects. It is a good idea to offer a few small insects from time to time throughout the rearing period even if little interest is initially shown in them.

An increase in the amount of multi-vitamins and minerals is beneficial and this should be dusted on to the livefood or another favoured item. A liquid vitamin supplement adheres better to livefood. A few birds have extremely specialised diets and these inevitably pose the greatest problems.

Hoopoes which in captivity are content to live virtually exclusively on maggots, need to have their moderate but nevertheless essential daily dose of multi-vitamins massively increased if the young are to develop properly. In particular vitamin D which converts calcium and phosphorus into bone, has to be supplied ceaselessly, as do vitamins A and E. Failure to provide the adult birds with their daily administrations of multi-vitamins and mineral salts, together with a drop per bird of concentrated vitamins A, D and E added to the maggots and mealworms of insectivorous birds such as hoopoes, which will not take inanimate food, will quickly result in a deterioration. This deterioration may not become apparent for some time—but is accompanied by a definite inability to form and lay eggs.

As with encouraging birds to breed in the first place, peace, quiet and seclusion are also essential to the rearing process. It is at this time that other birds in a communal aviary can be both directly and indirectly dangerous. Some seem to take malicious delight in destroying the nests of other birds, molesting their youngsters (although this can often stem from initial curiosity) and generally harrassing the mother. More understandably they also pinch all the choice extra foods which you put out specially for the family. Even so, it is by no means impossible to rear birds in such conditions (as was proved at Winged World)—it is just easier in separate accommodation.

However hard you strive to get everything just right, there will always be occasions—most experienced keepers will say far too many—when after all else has failed, the only course left to take is hand-rearing. With some kinds of birds, especially the larger seedeaters and fowl, this does not present too much of a problem but amongst softbills, only some of the omnivores present a reasonable chance of success. Some of the smaller insectivores are impossible to rear artificially with our current knowledge, and the same sadly goes for many of the larger ones too.

I feel sure the question of how to offer the food is as important as what to offer. Handling young birds causes them much distress and the manipulatory business of trying to get them to accept food greatly exacerbates the problem. This is certainly true in the early stages when the additional problem of keeping tiny naked nestlings at a constant temperature is extremely difficult—and handling them even more so.

It would not be wise to give lengthy advice here on how to hand-rear young softbills simply because I cannot guarantee to give the *right* advice. All I can recommend is that you think hard about the sort of food the parents would offer in the wild and try to simulate it as closely as possible.

The larger a nestling or fledgling is or grows, the easier theoretically it should be to rear, but all that usually happens is that one set of problems is replaced by another. By the time a bird grows to an age approaching independence, it has developed pretty firm ideas about what items it wants to eat and by who or what it wants them served up. There is an age somewhere between these two points—roughly speaking at about 6–10 days for most small to medium birds—when the nestling is more open to change but even then to start hand-rearing is by no means plain-sailing. Of course, the older a fledgling gets, the stronger it becomes and the more hope there is of it withstanding unnatural treatment.

The only softbills which I have frequently hand-reared with few problems are some of the medium-sized corvids, especially the Rook, Jackdaw and Magpie—and these flourish on a diet of turkey starter crumbs (which by definition contain all the requirements of fowl and therefore many other birds) moistened and formed into little pellets. Any bird large enough to be fed thus will stand a far better chance of surviving than on the traditional bread and milk. I have also reared sparrows, starlings and thrushes this way, and it is not only much more convenient but also cheaper than other methods.

The pigeon family is mainly a seedeating one and therefore not eligible for inclusion in this book but the fruit pigeons (and one or two others) are as their name implies, a different matter. Pigeons are fairly unique among birds in rearing their young (squabs) on a substance known as 'pigeons milk' produced in the parents' crop. Fruit pigeons seem to feed almost exclusively on fruit in the wild but their milk is highly nutritious and rich in protein—so much so that it could not be produced entirely from a diet of fruit, and certainly the buds and shoots consumed by the adult pigeons are an indispensable part of the squabs' diet too, as indeed they are of many other frugivores.

Apart from such easily neglected foods, we must never forget that the majority of softbills rear their young to a large extent on insects, as do a great many seedeaters. Mousebirds are one of the larger types to do so and so do most small nectivores. Some keepers on encountering difficulty in finding sufficient quantities of livefood release the parents to forage for themselves, only restraining them shortly before the young are due to leave the nest. This practice, quite admissable in theory, has obvious dangers but as a last resort can certainly be considered. A simple trapdoor let into the side or roof of the cage with a perch fitted nearby on both sides is all that is needed.

Six: Ailments

No matter how well they are cared for and how carefully they are fed, there is always the danger—even likelihood—that at some time or another one of your birds will become unwell. When this happens, it is imperative to act quickly. Softbills are no more prone to illness than any other type of bird; in fact it has been my experience in mixed collections for rather the opposite to be true—with parrots and birds-of-prey being the most troublesome. At the first sign that something is wrong, and a bird should not have to get seriously ill before we notice, remove it from its aviary to a hospital cage, which can be maintained at a temperature of 85°F (29.4°C). Warmth, a steady atmosphere, peace and subdued lighting are the basic requirements of all sick animals. These achieved, diagnosis and treatment can begin.

All animals in captivity have the infuriating habit of concealing their ailments for as long as possible; this defence mechanism serves them well in the wild—where the first sign of weakness generally means a speedy end—but works against them in captivity. However, a sympathetic eye quickly becomes trained to notice the slightest variation from the norm—however insignificant this might seem—and alerts you to danger. I have several times been stopped outside an aviary by the uneasy feeling that all is not well despite no obvious symptoms.

Hospital cages can be bought commercially or made at home from a box incorporating a glass front, sufficient ventilation holes and a simple electric light bulb either suspended above or hidden beneath a false floor to maintain the desired temperature at perch level. It is always best to isolate sick birds in case the ailment is infectious. Since sick birds are more likely to drink than eat, water must always be available and this can be provided in a glass, plastic or china dish into which multi-vitamins or antibiotics can be mixed. Given this preference for liquids, birds might be persuaded to take glucose or other forms of nutritious mixes (such as 'nectar'—*see* Chapter 3) when they would refuse solids.

For all serious injuries and diseases, breaks, fractures, deep wounds, eye and muscle disorders, a veterinary surgeon should be consulted. It is only sensible to consider home treatment if the complaint is a less serious one, easily diagnosed (such as a chill) or after much experience has been gained. Having said that, it is also true that you can greatly assist your veterinary doctor by describing the symptoms clearly and accurately on your first visit. As in describing a crime to the police, slight details which to you might seem unimportant, may unlock the door to the correct treatment.

One thing that all new bird-keepers should bear in mind is the risk of birds falling ill and dying no matter how much care and good treatment they get. The truth of the matter is that we do not yet know enough about avian psychology, and there are a number of bird diseases and disorders which are virtually undetectable in life, such as *Pasteurella pseudotuberculosis*. Post mortem examinations are strongly recommended whether the cause of death is known or not because only in this way is it possible to monitor exactly what is happening to your collection. It is always possible that an autopsy will reveal hitherto unsuspected conditions which might or might not have had anything to do with the actual fatality.

A regular laboratory analysis of the birds' droppings also gives a useful check on the health of the collection: giving early warning of infestations of worms and other endo-parasites.

As necessary and valuable as professional veterinarian care is, it must be said that most veterinarians have very little, if any, knowledge and experience of softbilled birds, especially foreign ones. It is important, therefore, that the serious keeper learns as much as he or she can about his or her charges and their most likely ailments so that the veterinarian can be guided along the right lines and thus prescribe the correct drugs which are so powerful nowadays that they do need expert control.

On page 49 is a short glossary of the most common problems to befall softbills but, I stress, with a good diet, hygienic care, attention to detail and a fair measure of luck, you will find most softbills amongst the most troublefree of all birds. Luck, as we have already seen, will play a major part in all your avicultural activities: with it, you can get away with all sorts of errors of judgement and achieve successes which, logically, should at least be improbable. On the other hand though, without luck, it will seem as if fate is against you however careful your husbandry, and there is little you can do except hope that your luck will change for the better.

Perhaps to a certain extent you help make your own luck. Certainly, I believe, that a good positive attitude rubs off on the birds: both in matters concerning breeding and health. As long as an animal has the will to live, it will cling stubbornly to life through the most adverse circumstances but, conversely, if it should give in, even if the condition is not yet terminal, there seems very little you can do to reverse the downward spiral. Hopefully, by flair and judicious, sensitive husbandry, such retrogression should never arise in the first place.

Birds which do fall ill and are removed to isolation should be attended to *after* the rest of the collection, and thereafter all utensils and your hands should be thoroughly washed. If, after a bird has been placed in a hospital cage, it shows no improvement after 24 hours, professional advice should be sought without further delay. But sometimes even 24 hours delay can be critical and if in any doubt help should be summoned immediately. The following list of complaints include only those that are more easily detected: any bird showing signs of lethargy or strange behaviour should be regarded critically. The usual signs of illness are discharges, diarrhoea, inflammation, constipation, bleeding, visible swellings and plumage disorders.

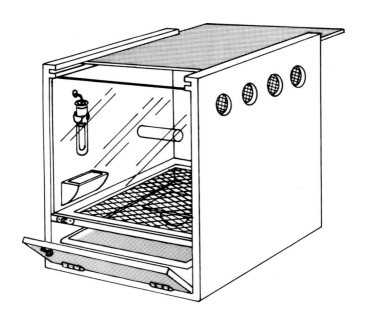

Hospital cage

Abscess, a bacterial infection which can be successfully treated with antibiotics.

Anaemia is characterized by dejection and listlessness; its cause is usually a result of tuberculosis (*see* **Avian tuberculosis**), Red Mite (*see* **Mites**) or internal parasites (*see* **Worms**).

Aspergillosis is a disease, usually fatal, caused by fungal infection of the lungs and air sacs through inhalation of *Aspergillus fumigatus* spores which can be present in any decaying vegetation. There is no known cure but preventive measures include lacing drinking water with potassium iodide to the strength of 30 grams per pint.

Avian tuberculosis cannot be positively diagnosed in life, and even if it could be, there is no known treatment. Affected birds are emaciated and listless, becoming progressively worse. Complete sterilisation of the aviary should be carried out.

Broken and damaged limbs should be treated *at once* preferably by a professional veterinarian. Home doctoring can do more harm than good: speed is essential and by the time a mistake is noticed, it is usually too late to do anything about it. Dislocation and compound fractures are prone to infection and several more complications.

Coccidiosis can be triggered by stress after the coccidia *Escherichia coli* has lain dormant for many years, indeed, many otherwise healthy birds carry it throughout life with no ill effects. Infected birds show dejection, loose feathering, vomiting, diarrhoea (often blood-stained) and ingest much grit. If a prompt diagnosis is made effective treatment with one of the modern sulpha drugs is possible.

Common cold cannot be caught by birds but an infection of the upper respiratory tract called **Coryza** is the nearest avian equivalent. Symptoms are a discharge from the eyes and nostrils. If left untreated, the condition can spread to the lungs, becoming chronic and leading to pneumonia which results in rapid breathing, wheezing and sneezing. Isolation and professional care are essential—which will include a course of antibiotics.

Conjunctivitis is an infection of the eyes first revealed by watering; if untreated, the affected eye(s) becomes closed, swollen and often matted with dirt and feathers. Professional care is advised if early treatment with Golden Eye Ointment or something similar is unsuccessful. Blindness can result.

Constipation is a symptom rather than an illness and most often caused by incorrect feeding. More greenfood and vitamin B solve a mild bout but it might be necessary to dose with olive oil or liquid paraffin if things do not improve.

Convulsions which can be fatal are often caused by apoplexy— obesity, lack of exercise and an incorrect diet. A haemorrhage causes paralysis in the legs or wings but if treated quickly with Epsom salts combined with a low protein diet, a cure is possible. It is not a condition likely to occur in birds housed in a large aviary and fed correctly.

Cysts and skin tumours—such growths should be treated with an astringent like tincture of iodine or friars balsam, lanced with a sterile scalpel and gently relieved, however if in any doubt consult your veterinarian.

Diarrhoea is, like constipation, symptomatic of many illnesses but not one in itself. Remember that softbills because of the nature of their food have very loose droppings to begin with, but those which are very watery can be due simply to bad food, an incorrect diet or dirty utensils. If nothing of this sort is suspected, professional advice—due to the complexity of the problem—must be sought, but be prepared for disappointment because many of the diseases causing diarrhoea can only be identified after death.

Egg-binding is rarely a problem with softbills but if a bird is looking wretched, hunched on the floor and periodically straining, further examination might well reveal a swelling just inside the cloaca or vent. The patient should immediately be placed in a warm room—if this together with annointing the area with liquid paraffin or glycerine and introducing olive oil gently into the cloaca does not help the bird to pass the blocked egg, she should be assisted by very tenderly probing the area while being held over a bowl of steaming water. Care must be taken not to break the egg. By this time the bird will be very weak and she must be allowed to convalesce in a warm environment. Egg-binding mostly occurs with the first egg of the season, in cold weather, with young birds or, of course, with oversized eggs. However, with a well balanced diet including plenty of calcium, it is not likely to occur.

Enteritis is inflammation of the intestines and can be caused by bad food or an infection. Many diseases including **Coccidiosis** can cause enteritis which is accompanied by diarrhoea, greenish in colour. Professional advice must be sought.

Feather lice live in and on the feathers of birds causing skin irritations and harsh brittle feathers. Dusting with pyrethrum powder or one of the modern sprays quickly cures the problem— which is not nearly so prevalent as it used to be.

Gapes, which involves coughing and strained breathing with mouth wide open accompanied by awful wheezing in severe cases, is caused by a lung parasite called *Syngamus trachealis*. The condition is highly infectious since the eggs are coughed up from the trachea, swallowed and passed out to the aviary floor where they are picked up by other birds. Under professional treatment, this condition can be eradicated although once a bird is infected, it can be difficult to cure. I have successfully treated Choughs—which along with starlings seem particularly susceptible to gapeworm—with the old-fashioned gamekeepers' trick of inserting a soft feather soaked in paraffin down the windpipe (avoiding the pharynx)—this causes the bird to cough up the troublesome eggs.

Mites, especially the Red Mite (*Dermanyssus gallinae*), are one of the most common causes of anaemia and listlessness in softbills. The Red Mite is a blood-sucker which usually spends the day in the nest or crevice, venturing out at night to attack the birds. Treatment should be prompt and consist of dusting or spraying the victim with an insecticide, vacating the cage or aviary during the day and thoroughly sterilizing it.

The annual Moult. Any bird showing signs of having moult problems should be removed to a hospital cage, fed well and encouraged to keep quiet. It is not a problem for birds on a good diet.

Ornithosis is a serious virus disease most often encountered in newly-imported stock. If diagnosed at an early stage it can be at least partially treated by antibiotics. Symptoms resemble those of a severe cold or even pneumonia, but many birds carry the disease without showing signs of it. It is certainly endemic in Britain.

Overgrown beak and claws, rare in aviary birds, are most frequently seen in caged birds perching on slim machined-dowelling. It is only a minor problem but one which requires attention. On trimming, the cut must be made avoiding the blood vessel to prevent severe bleeding. The vein becomes visible if the claw or beak is held up to the light.

Examples of overgrown beak and claws;
--- cut to be made here

Pasteurelosis (*Pasteurella pseudotuberculosis*) is a common pathogen in some areas and particularly evil because of its sudden and fatal consequences. In my experience, a cold dry winter helps to keep it at bay but it is difficult to combat. Scrupulous hygiene and wholesome food and water help, but it is equally important to discourage wild birds from contaminating outside aviaries. Do not be tempted to introduce rodents such as guinea pigs in an attempt to keep grass down since all rodents can carry fatal avian diseases. The rapid drainage of rain-water also helps to keep aviaries healthy.

Rickets is generally caused by an imbalance of the calcium/phosphorus ratio in the diet; it is fairly common in young softbills—especially insectivores—and is revealed by a deformity in the legs. A close watch should be kept for any such deformity and instant remedial action taken by increasing the calcium in the diet. Calcium lactate tablets can be obtained from the chemist, and in severe cases, veterinary surgeons can give doses of Vitamin D_3. With experience, the onset of rickets-like diseases can be anticipated and prevented by judicious enhancement of the parents' diet before hatching.

Salmonellosis caused by the *Salmonella* bacteria attacks many birds and is symptomised by white coloured diarrhoea, a dejected appearance, excessive thirst—in short, dysentery—and very often a matted ventral region. Laboratory examination of the droppings must be done at once. It can be contracted from mammals such as rodents or, indeed, other birds, and can be passed on to humans.

Scaly leg, face and beak are caused by a small mite (*Cnemidocoptes pilae*) and are betrayed by yellowish encrustations. It is seldom a problem with softbills, and is not difficult to cure: the flaky crust should be removed and burnt, and a 10% solution of benzyl benzoate applied to the exposed area for a few days.

Thrush, also called **Pox** and **Canker**, is a form of avian diptheria occurring as cheesy lesions in the mouth and throat. Birds often conceal the condition until it is too late but if it is suspected, a veterinarian must be summoned immediately.

Worms in the form of roundworms and tapeworms can infest softbills although roundworms are the most common and easiest to clear. Analysis of droppings can prevent the condition from becoming chronic, but even if whole worms are found in the droppings a cure can be effected by treatment with one of the Piperazine compounds although it takes Thiabenzole to tackle tapeworms. If in doubt, consult your veterinarian.

Seven: The Softbills

Aviculturally, softbills are best classified by their feeding preferences: frugivores (fruit-eaters), insectivores (insect-eaters), nectivores (nectar-eaters), omnivores, which take a broad range of all kinds of food, and a few fringe carnivores. This chapter begins with those generally considered the most adaptable and works through to the group containing the most difficult birds—the insectivores—at the end. It is important to remember that there are 'easy' and 'difficult' types within each group, and that most softbills are really omnivores with specific leanings towards one or another group but it is convenient to split them thus, providing we do not follow the categories slavishly. For greater details of diets the previous chapters should be consulted as well.

Barbet

Toucan

Hummingbird

Bee-eater

Kingfisher

OMNIVORES

In many respects STARLINGS are the typical omnivores and as such among the best of all softbills—not only for the beginner, but equally for the more discerning aviculturist since among their number are such birds as the endangered Rothschild's Starling or Grackle and other rare and little known mynahs from SE Asia. 'Mynah' or 'myna' is a substantive name applied to many Asian starlings.

The one softbill known to just about everybody on account of its powers of mimicry is the Greater Hill Mynah. Small cages are totally unsuited to this large, active, intelligent and gregarious bird; it is much better off in a roomy planted aviary for your own sake too, on account of its messy habits. However, if you are the owner of a pet mynah and do not wish to go to the trouble or expense of obtaining a mate and building an aviary, there is no need to worry: mynahs can be kept healthy and fairly happy in such a cage, it is just that ideally they deserve something more. Male and female are alike in plumage, so obtaining a true pair can be difficult.

There are several smaller mynahs, all of which make delightful avicultural subjects. The Common, Bank, Malabar, Pagoda or Brahminy and Lesser or Southern Hill Mynahs are the commonest and, because they do not imitate the human voice, are very much cheaper. The Black-winged Starling or Grackle—which looks a bit like a small Rothschild's—and the Asian Green Starling are two good Asiatic species which are not often called mynahs. Starlings and mynahs alike should be fed on fruit, softfood and a certain amount of livefood especially when rearing young—a task undertaken by both parents. They also enjoy all manner of extras.

Starlings are well represented in Africa, and provide many superb aviary birds, notably the glossy starlings which have resplendent plumage covered by the most marvellous irridescence. Supreme amongst the glossy starlings are the Superb Spreo, Long-tailed, Bristle-crowned and Royal Starlings; of which the first mentioned is the most commonly available and easily bred. The Green (Blue-eared) and Purple Glossy Starlings are cheaper and well suited to mix in flocks in large aviaries—a policy which encourages breeding.

Most starlings while mixing fairly well amongst themselves tend to be aggressive to other similarly sized species especially when

Superb tanager

Red-whiskered bulbul

Superb spreo

Hunting cissa

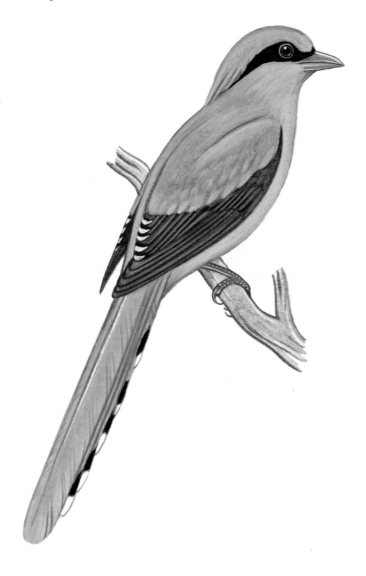

breeding. The Superb Spreo and Violet-backed Starlings are the least aggressive of all. Among the mynahs, the Common is possibly the best mixer. You can quite often judge their demeanour from outward appearance: the larger, stronger looking members of this group are usually the most dangerous.

The Violet-backed and Wattled Starlings are more insectivorous than the remainder and also less hardy and less inclined to breed. All starlings require artificial shelters into which they can retreat at night and in bad weather, but however cold the weather, only a few require artificial heat. The Violet-backed Starling is one which possibly does. Almost without exception, starlings are hole-nesters and must be provided with large amounts of nesting material.

As with the preceding group, the only adverse feature of CORVIDS in captivity is their aggressiveness towards other birds. This effectively means that pairs of crows, jays and magpies for instance, have to be given their own exclusive accommodation. Fortunately they are larger than life, and any aviary housing a pair has no need for a supporting cast.

Jays and magpies (including those varieties known as treepies) are the most popular species because of their smaller size, slightly daintier ways and more attractive plumage and voice. The treepies are the least dangerous of all crows but it is still dangerous to mix them with any bird not able to stand up for itself.

The Indian Treepie also called the Wandering and Rufous Treepie is one of the most desirable species: it is beautifully garbed in shades of tan and grey, and has one of the most delightful calls of all birds—a melodious, warbling, bubbling trill. Some of the other small magpies are also highly recommended, the Azure-winged Magpie in particular is a beauty—one of the very few which can be mixed with other types owing to its quiet ways and docile temperament. Of the larger magpies, the Red-billed Magpie is a familiar incumbent of many zoos and bird gardens. It is easy to look after, very tough and, like a great many of its tribe, willing to breed while being infamous for its habit of eating its own offspring. To stand a chance of rearing the young, a surfeit of livefood of as many kinds as possible must be *constantly* available. The Yellow-billed Magpie is similar in most respects but less common.

The Common Magpie is a familiar sight to European birdwatchers but nonetheless beautiful for that, and it makes a good aviary inhabitant. More exotic and, indeed, common in British collections is the Green Magpie or Hunting Cissa which, if housed and fed correctly retains its beautiful green plumage; however, if prevented from skulking in dense cover, the green fades to blue in direct sunshine. This happens even to Wild Cissas living in more open country.

Jays are renowned for their exquisite plumage and engaging personalities which can, all too easily, seduce one into regarding them with less than due caution. There is no doubt that jays—even amongst themselves—are some of the most territorial and dangerous of all birds, and should not on any account be mixed with other sorts. For all that, there are some species which crave attention providing you have the space and facilities available.

Apart from the Eurasian Jay which is in itself a marvellous subject, the Lanceolated Jay from Central Asia and the Pileated and Green Jays both from the New World, are perhaps those best known. The Old World species are hardiest but like the magpies have the infuriating habit of destroying their own young. Apart from the necessary livefood when the young hatch, jays eat all sorts of food and in particular love acorns, nuts and some fruit, quite apart from animal protein.

Crows in captivity require a certain amount of roughage in their diet and this is best provided in the form of 'white' mice or rats and chicks. But they are easy to look after and it is very perplexing why the true crows are so little kept and evidently not highly regarded by many aviculturists. Birds such as the Jackdaw, Raven and Hooded Crow are ideal aviary subjects and it is a great pity that more are not kept. Some African species—such as the Pied Crow—do appear occasionally but they are the exceptions. The Chough with its striking red bill and legs, and the Alpine Chough in which the red is replaced by yellow, are daintier representatives and the former is decreasing alarmingly in the wild. A co-ordinated captive breeding policy could help avert its complete demise but already they are hard to acquire being quite rightly protected in Britain at least.

More specialized corvids are the nutcrackers which, as their name implies, are more akin to hardbills—feeding almost exclusively on pine seeds and nuts etc.—but again they are rare in aviculture.

The larger members of the rather arbitrary SONG-BABBLERS group should be regarded separately to the other babblers which are more insectivorous in their habits. Some of the most important song-babblers, better known as jay-thrushes or laughing-thrushes, are the White-crested and Necklaced Laughing-thrushes: both of which are straightforward to maintain if highly belligerent towards other similarly-sized species. There are nearly 50 species of *Garrulax* laughing-thrushes but few are ever seen in aviaries; the Red-headed Laughing-thrush is one which is quite the opposite to those mentioned above, being docile and self-effacing.

One of the few softbills which is frequently kept in cages is the Pekin Robin, alternatively named (by dealers in search of the exotic) Red-billed Leiothrix and Pekin or Japanese Nightingale. It is a favourite with many beginners on account of its easy-going nature, attractive character and simple maintenance. Kept in a communal aviary, its one disadvantage is its partiality to the eggs of other birds. Closely-related and similar in most respects is the Silver-eared Mesia, also from Asia. Both species are surprisingly tough and appreciate a small amount of seed mixed into their softfood, as do the corvids.

There should be no mistaking the evil intent of most jay-thrushes, and on no account should they be mixed even with far larger birds from which it is hoped to breed, because of their confirmed and expert depradations of nests and their contents. Any injured bird, even one of their own kind, is also fair game. Kept on their own though, they are superb.

Regarding breeding, they are unreliable—often showing no interest at all—this must often be due to the fact that the lack of sexual dimorphism results in pairs of the same sex living together.

First rate subjects for the beginner, BULBULS are vivacious lively songsters which are easy to keep and generally hardy once acclimatised. The Asian species such as the Red-vented, White-cheeked and Red-whiskered (-eared) are most regularly available to British enthusiasts than those from Africa, but all require spacious planted enclosures if they are to breed. Although occasionally quarrelsome, they can with care be kept in mixed aviaries.

Bulbuls are truly omnivorous: eating whatever small animal food they can get, and supplementing this with berries and seeds. A good insectile-mix together with a little fruit, a generous amount of livefood and anything else available will keep them hale and hearty in captivity. There are well over 100 species and they occur in the wild over an extremely wide range of habitats from suburban gardens, deserts, and tropical rain forests. Evidently highly adaptable, they are amongst the most reliable softbill breeders. Plenty of twigs and dried grass should be supplied and maybe a solid foundation of some sort.

Similar in many ways to the bulbuls but more frugivorous and far fewer in number, one or two of the LEAFBIRDS are common in softbill collections. Best known are the fruitsuckers or chloropsis (from their scientific name)—in particular the Golden-fronted and to a lesser extent the Hardwick's Fruitsuckers. The only other oft-kept species is the stunning Fairy Bluebird—which is becoming more and more common as its price drops; it is one of two comprising the *Irena* genus.

The remaining genus—*Aegithina*—consists of four ioras; they are seen only rarely, being seldom imported, and are virtually entirely insectivorous. They are less hardy than the others, all of which should have frostproof winter quarters available.

Fruitsuckers and bluebirds can be dangerous to other birds when in breeding condition but are generally peaceful enough at other times. They are all immensely attractive: the fruitsuckers in shades of green with black, orange or blue facial markings. The male Fairy Bluebird is resplendent in glossy black and irridescent waxy ultramarine. Members of this group can be given a nectar mix if desired and insects when they are plentiful or when young are being reared. Mealworms are also used for bringing such birds into final breeding condition.

In the wild (SE Asia) leafbirds are gregarious inhabitants of forested country where they roam looking for fruiting trees in the company of birds as dissimilar as hornbills, lories (nectar-feeding parrots) and fruit pigeons.

TANAGERS are some of the most popular, colourful and frequently imported of all softbills. Not surprisingly with such a large family (some 230 species occur in South America), there are numerous sorts available to the aviculturist, of which Mrs. Wilson's (Masked or Golden-masked) and the Silver-throated Tanagers are two of the hardiest and most familiar. Aviculturists contemplating specialization in tanagers should remember that more males than females are usually imported, and that it might take a while for true pairs to be realized, although breeding prospects are ultimately good.

Other tough species are the one or two North American members of the *Piranga* genus and the *Thraupis* blue and palm tanagers. The Blue-grey (Blue or Silver-blue) is one of the best known of all. Although for a different reason, with sexually alike species like this, it might also take some time for a true pair to be obtained. One or two of the larger tanagers including this one can be very disruptive to other nesting birds. The large Magpie and Black Tanagers are a couple more which have to be housed with caution—although at times they are perfectly peaceable.

No southern tanager should be subjected to a temperature below freezing and several are significantly less hardy, among them the Spotted Emerald (Speckled) and Superb (Seven-coloured) Tanagers, and these should be avoided by all inexperienced tanager keepers since they are also very tricky to acclimatize. The Superb in particular is prone to digestive disorders. Many people make the mistake of offering tanagers only cultivated soft fruit, forgetting they are true omnivores. Soft fruit is important but they must also have soaked dried fruit, softfood with added minced meat and some livefood; the larger types will also consume carrion.

Far less frequently imported and therefore more expensive are the smaller principally frugivorous tanagers, the chlorophonias and euphonias. The Blue-crowned Chlorophonia is the species most often seen; all four are greenish birds enlivened by blue or yellow about the head. They are tricky to acclimatize and thereafter need a very varied fruit diet inclusive of some nectar. On the credit side, they are active and sociable, safe to house with all other non-aggressive softbills in roomy planted enclosures where they should be protected from extremes of cold. They are rain-bathers.

Euphonias—personified in some British collections by the Violet Euphonia or Tanager—are also lively, small and gaily-coloured, and should be treated similarly.

A few of the rarer and lesser known BARBETS are thought to live mainly on fruit but so far as we are here concerned, barbets can be regarded very much as omnivores. They are noisy, entertaining and hardy providing they have access to nestboxes for roosting in, or an old upright log in which they can excavate their own with their immensely powerful beaks. Indeed, the smaller species can perish overnight if forced to roost outside in cold weather. Most barbets are willing to breed—again in a chamber they have excavated for themselves—and at such times they become fiercely territorial.

Several frequently appear in even quite modest collections. The Blue-throated or Blue-cheeked Barbet, regularly exported from India, is large (23 cm long) and smartly clad in the typical green with red and blue about the head. Less frequently coming from the same country is the Coppersmith Barbet—a smaller species and rather less hardy. It is also frugivorous in inclination but a good general purpose barbet diet is 50% softfood (with minced meat added) and 25% each of livefood and fruit.

There are more barbets from Africa than anywhere else but none is as common as those emanating from India. The little D'Arnaud's Barbet is unusual in that given the opportunity it will burrow into a bank or even vertically down into the soil to construct its nesting chamber. The Double-toothed Barbet is another occasional species coming from Africa, and considerably larger and more pugnacious. The diminutive tinkerbirds are also from Africa but not recommended to beginners despite their strange and beguiling voices. A better bet is the Red-fronted Barbet which can be safely housed with smaller softbills.

Even rarer in European aviaries are the New World barbets of which the well-named Toucan Barbet is a fine example. It has striking looks and a robust character which demands separate accommodation. Both sexes are superbly coloured but they can be split by the males' black stripe down the hind-neck. The Black-spotted and Red-headed Barbets are also exported from South America but nowadays less and less frequently.

By far the best representative in aviculture of the robust, territorial American TYRANT FLYCATCHERS is the Great Kiskadee or Derbian Flycatcher. It is about as far-removed from the normal idea of a flycatcher as could be imagined, even painfully attacking its keeper when nesting—which it indulges in readily if provided with a nestbox. The young are easy to rear providing the adults have an omnivorous diet including fruit, strips of lean meat or fish, livefood and a rich softfood. Indeed, it has many kingfisher-like habits and bathes by flying directly into a pool.

The NEW WORLD ORIOLES are more diverse and important to aviculture than their Old World namesakes. Best known in Europe are the cowbirds, marshbirds, meadowlarks and the Troupial. One species, variously called the Military Starling, Red-breasted Marshbird, Long-tailed Meadowlark and Patagonian Marsh Starling should not be confused with the Lesser Red-breasted Meadowlark and the Red-breasted Blackbird which are also called 'military-starlings'. Perhaps the easiest way of avoiding this plethora is to always quote its scientific name, *Sturnella loyca*.

The meadowlarks and marshbirds are attractive confiding birds requiring a varied diet of softfood, fruit, livefood, some carrion and even seeds for some. On account of their size it is safest to mix them only with equally strong species although they are not especially aggressive. The Shiny Cowbird (also described as the Silky, Glossy and Common) and its five close relatives seem to be aspiring cuckoos in that they often lay their eggs in other birds nests.

The OLD WORLD ORIOLES are less important and it is surprising that the beautifully coloured Golden Oriole occurring across such a wide range through the Palearctic, Ethiopian and Oriental zoogeographical regions is not more often seen in collections. It is left to the Black-naped and Black-headed Orioles mainly from SE Asia to fly the flag. Female orioles are generally duller than the males. They are true omnivores, hardy but fairly peaceful although they should not be mixed with any bird unable to stand up for itself.

HORNBILLS are amongst the most evocative of all tropical birds but in aviculture only the smaller more insectivorous species are at all suitable for the hobbyist. The larger sorts present problems of space, facilities and commitment that will be beyond all save the experienced aviculturist and specialist.

By and large there are three size categories of hornbills. Spectacularly large, the Great Pied and Rhinoceros Hornbills (two of three *Buceros* species) and the Helmeted Hornbill all from the Far East are primarily zoo birds where the space and professional expertise are on hand. They are deadly to most small birds—swallowing many whole. The huge and grotesquely charming ground hornbills are also only suitable for zoos and parkland.

Even the medium-sized group which includes many of the typical hornbills such as the Tarictic, and the various pied, casqued and crested species are too dangerous to mix with any bird of similar or smaller size. All these birds will eat a variety of foods, inanimate as well as animate but they have a definite preference for substantial small vertebrates like small mammals, birds, reptiles and amphibians.

It is the group of smaller *Tockus* hornbills which are of most interest to the amateur softbill keeper. Within this genus are the Red-billed, Yellow-billed, Von der Decken's, Crowned and Common Grey Hornbills. All hornbills require considerable space in which to fly about but the Red-billed Hornbill is one which can be easily managed in a smaller flight-cage. Being essentially insectivorous, these smaller birds can be safely housed with quite small softbills if so desired. Apart from livefood, they should also be given a little fruit, red meat and softfood. I have found them susceptible to frost damage—even to the extent of losing toes—and so are best shut into a shed at night in the winter.

The hornbills' breeding cycle including the incarceration of the female in the nest chamber is by now fairly well known. In captivity, hornbills readily accept nestboxes of suitable dimensions and providing mud is supplied, stand a good chance of breeding successfully. The male bird plays a vital role in helping to seal in his mate and thereafter feeding her (for 30–50 days) and later, hopefully, their offspring which can be as many as five in number until the female breaks out after an equivalent length of time. The young are then resealed in and fed by both parents for the short period until they too are ready to leave. The nesting material which has been stacked into the chamber does not as might be expected become the least soiled, because the incarcerated birds direct their droppings through the slit opening. The female makes use of the incubation period for undergoing a complete moult.

Seldom thought of as softbills, certain kinds of the large pigeon family quite apart from the fruit pigeons are equally due such classification. Best known of the GROUND DOVES to zoo visitors are the crowned pigeons (*Goura*) of Papua, New Guinea— large and spectacular terrestrial birds which live on fruit, softfood and livefood as well as some seeds. They roost in trees and also nest off the ground—when they can become aggressive to their aviary companions.

The true ground doves (*Gallicolumba*) are best known by the bleeding-heart pigeons from the Philippines which have a fairly good record of breeding in captivity. They require fruit and insectile additives to what is basically a granivorous diet. While certainly quite hardy, they should be protected from severe frosts.

The quail-doves (*Geotrygon*) which include the desirable Mountain Witch Dove of Jamaica are less tough and should be given cosy winter quarters. Their diet is similar to that of the crowned pigeons.

Ten out of the fourteen BROADBILLS are Asian, the others are African but only one of the whole family is at all familiar—the Lesser Green Broadbill—a fact almost certainly due to its willingness to take fruit which makes it a better investment for trappers and easier to acclimatize than the more insectivorous species. Unfortunately, like a great many tropical species which show marked sexual dimorphism, only the brighter coloured males are generally bothered with by the trappers who presumably eat the females, and I have yet to see one; perhaps one day they will get up to date. All broadbills are gentle and retiring—ideal for mixing with other small softbills. But they must be offered insectile food and a small amount of livefood if they are to remain in good condition.

Supreme among those symbols of the tropics, the South American COTINGAS, are two species of cock-of-the-rocks—one red, the other orange. In recent years their price has dropped from former exorbitant levels but they are still very expensive. Perhaps surprisingly, they are hardy, straightforward to maintain and provide a not hopeless breeding challenge, but their aggressive tendencies cannot be ignored.

Few of the smaller cotingas are offered with any consistency. The Orange-breasted Cotinga is sometimes seen but all are to be recommended because of their many virtues. Acclimatization can be a problem with South American stock but nowadays this seldom concerns the amateur.

There are a few other elite omnivorous birds such as the enchanting but temperamental little MANAKINS (Pipridae) also from the New World. Only the Blue-backed and, to a lesser degree, the Long-tailed Manakins are available with any frequency but even these two require specialist treatment. They should not be allowed to live totally on fruit but encouraged to eat some softfood, small insects and *a little* nectar. They should be housed in a group—another factor working against them—and are ideally suited to heated conservatories or tropical houses, although a well sheltered outdoor aviary with heated winter quarters could well prove to be best of all. Manakins have a unique courtship behaviour which involves a dance around vertical twigs on a cleared piece of land.

The famous BIRDS-OF-PARADISE and BOWERBIRDS are no longer available to aviculturists; if they were, many old-fashioned beliefs about them would have to be changed. In many respects they are indeed very similar to crows: tough, highly omnivorous with definite carnivorous tendencies and not at all the hothouse flowers nor the exclusive vegetarians they were so long believed to be.

FRUGIVORES

Although only a relatively small family, the African TURACOS (or touracos) are important to aviculture. They are the most suitable purely frugivorous species and deserving of a greater degree of specialization than so far granted them. Like all frugivores they are necessarily arboreal, agile and active. In addition, the turacos are seldom exceeded in sheer beauty: they display a quality of plumage and poise that make even their stationary aspect enchanting, and once in flight, alternately dipping and gliding to reveal their startling magenta wing speculums, they become quite breathtaking.

The White-cheeked Turaco is the most widespread type in captivity and the only one regularly bred but several more are also encountered, notably the White-headed, Pink-crested, Hartlaub's, Livingstone's and Purple-crested Turacos of the smaller ones. They are all basically of green plumage with violaceous touches about the tail and wings, the species are differentiated largely by the ornamentation on the head, in particular the design of the crest.

The slightly larger plantain-eaters have a darker violet plumage and very colourful facial markings; the Lady Ross's or Violet Turaco is the best known. Much less colourful in shades of grey and white are the louries or go-away birds (so called from their cry) with the Grey Lourie being advertised most frequently.

Largest of the turacos is the Great Blue Turaco—half as long again as the smaller varieties. It is a stately bird and becoming more accessible in recent years as the price decreases a little. It is likely though in the near future for all African countries to become less willing to permit the exploitation of their indigenous fauna, and so an all-out effort is needed to breed from those already in collections.

Turacos can be mixed with other softbills providing there is plenty of space including a long clear flight path and one or two clambering areas. Due to their monogamy and lack of sexual dimorphism quarrels are common but even well-mated pairs occasionally fight each other. Nests are flimsy pigeon-like structures and require some support. Two white eggs are laid which hatch in about 20 days. One of the biggest problems encountered in rearing the chicks is their susceptibility to a rickets-like leg deformity which needs massive doses of calcium to prevent or correct it.

Sulphur breasted toucan

Emerald toucanet

Bohemian waxwing

Blue-naped mousebird

Cuviers toucan

Knysna touraco (*Tauraco corythaix*)

The addition of an insectile-mix and some greenfood to the basic fruit diet will keep them in good condition although they will accept many other items including cheese, hard-boiled egg, buds, flowers and even insects especially when rearing young.

Mainly frugivorous but certainly in need of some animal protein and a broadly-based diet, the TOUCANS from the South American rainforests are probably the most distinctive and spectacular of all softbill families. But despite their undeniable glamour they must be viewed with circumspection by all those with less than zoos at their disposal. They are expensive but straightforward to look after, and they should not be housed anywhere which does not take into account their large size, high arboreal habits, poor flight and antagonism towards other birds and even their own kind at times.

The Sulphur-breasted, Cuvier's and Toco Toucans are the most familiar large members of the 38 recorded species. Smaller and more suitable to the amateur are the toucanets especially the Emerald Toucanet. Requiring conventional toucan care including dry winter night quarters, the toucanets can be happily mixed with many medium-sized softbills. Toucans are not delicate but object to the cold when it is accompanied by wind and rain. Unfortunately, the aracaris are also irritable inhabitants of a communal aviary and just as dangerous to smaller birds as the toucans.

Breeding toucans is not as improbable as it might seem providing pairs are well-mated and a suitable nestbox is present. Some notable successes have occurred in America and Germany, and all the signs suggest that once hatched, the young are not hard to rear.

The FRUIT PIGEONS from SE Asia deserve to be more popular than they are on account of their highly attractive looks and simple management. Their main requirements are plenty of fruit, a little softfood and roomy, warm and well-planted quarters. They are not in the least aggressive except to their own kind when nesting and are therefore ideal for mixed aviaries. Being exceptionally lazy birds, they tend to obesity unless their diet is strictly controlled and they are forced to exercise by at least travelling up and down to their food dish which should be placed on the floor as far from a perch as possible. All pigeons are inveterate bathers but will not use standing water, so if housed inside they must be sprayed; outside in dry weather, they love having the spray of a hosepipe played over them and stretch out one wing then the other luxuriously so that both upper and lower surfaces get thoroughly drenched.

So called because of their colour and habit of scurrying about the branches, the African MOUSEBIRDS or colies have crests, long tails and sharply clawed toes. They are highly gregarious outside the breeding season and often roost in clusters hanging vertically down, suspended by their outer toes which can be directed either forwards or backwards.

Their common names are self-descriptive: Blue-naped, White-headed, White-backed, Red-backed, Red-faced and Speckled. The first mentioned being most commonly available. As a group they ought to be more popular; among their assets are a friendly disposition, easy management, willingness to breed, entertaining natures and an abundant status in the wild. If housed in densely planted aviaries, and fed on a mainly frugivorous diet inclusive of some animal protein and softfood, no trouble should be encountered with them.

The popular WAXWINGS are agile, gentle and sociable, suitable for mixed aviaries. The Bohemian Waxwing occurs on both sides of the Atlantic; of the two other species making up the *Bombycilla* genus, one is Japanese, the other American. The adults feed mainly on fruit and berries but the young require much insect-life.

NECTIVORES

The WHITE-EYES or zosterops occur across a wide part of the Old World, there are nearly 80 species but as is usual it is the species from India which are imported most frequently. They are the best choice for the emerging nectar-feeder specialist since they are fairly cheap and reasonably hardy. Well-mated pairs will go down to nest in conservatories and any aviary which has sufficiently luxuriant vegetation but the young are difficult to rear. They consume many aphids and other plant pests but cause much damage in fruit-growing areas and in captivity sometimes destroy the buds and shoots of small plants. These natural tendencies illustrate their correct captive diet: nectar with some soft fruit and insects.

Providing you are organised to deal with them, the shimmering SUNBIRDS are much simpler to keep than most beginners assume. They are more obviously nectivorous than the white-eyes and require similar treatment to the hummingbirds of the New World which they replace east of the Atlantic Ocean, although they are less mobile and have to have their food placed in dishes or fountains accessible from a perch. They are tougher than they look, but must be shielded from severe weather, and are therefore best housed in conservatories, tropical houses, or best of all, indoor pens with planted outside flights.

Sunbirds are equally difficult to mix both with their own kind and other small birds such as the hummingbirds but the injury they can cause is directly proportional to their increased size and strength; and they are only marginally easier to breed. Some males assume a duller female-like plumage out of the breeding season but most species display pronounced sexual dimorphism.

Although certainly confirmed nectivores, sunbirds are by no means exclusively so and some species in particular consume large numbers of insects especially those which do not migrate in the dry season. In captivity, they all enjoy a small amount of sweet fruit and this can be supplied as orange segments or grape-halves spiked on twigs, or soaked sultanas.

Happily, quite a few sunbirds are to be seen in European collections. As regards behaviour, they tend to fall into two groups: 'wedge-tails' which are easier to manage and mix and the less co-operative 'long-tails.' In size they vary considerably from the large Malachite Sunbird (a long-tail) at 25.5 cm down to the tiny Asiatic Van Hasselt's (a wedge-tail)—at slightly less than 10 cm—and the fractionally larger Variable Sunbird, another wedge-tail. There are several races of this charming sunbird, and it is available at a fair price on account of its wide distribution in East Africa.

The moult is a demanding time for all birds but the smaller varieties have it particularly hard. The Beautiful Sunbird, a long-tailed African species, has a poor reputation for succumbing in moults but a close watch should be kept on all sunbirds.

One of the largest wedge-tailed species is the African Scarlet-chested Sunbird—a lively, eye-catching bird which is often fed on artificial colour-food to help the male retain its colouring. It frequently shows interest in nesting if its flight is well planted but the male often becomes too antagonistic towards the female and has to be removed.

The Malachite and Tacazze Sunbirds are vigorous long-tailed African species which make up for their lack of distinctive

Variable sunbird

Scarlet chested sunbird

Bee hummingbird

Bananaquit

Red legged honeycreeper

Indian zosterop (*Zosterpos palpebrosa*)

markings by their stunning irridescence. It is not possible to say which sunbirds are most likely to breed; I suspect that any well-mated pair might attempt to do so. Once again, thorough research and attention to detail reveal all sorts of important clues to correct management.

Tropical birds time their breeding to coincide with the season when food is at its most plentiful. This may be a fruiting or flowering period or, as is the case with many birds which require quantities of insects, during or soon after the rainy season. And it was very noticeable with a pair of Tacazze Sunbirds I looked after (and which eventually bred successfully) that their stimulus to start nest-building coincided exactly with the activating of a submersible pump after a winter's inactivity, which caused water to fall over rocks. They constructed their pendulous nest over the running water and it closely resembled flood debris caught on an overhanging branch and was only revealed as a nest when the water level dropped. This is quite a common means of camouflage and one that is also followed by the manakins. It might well be that running water proves to be an essential element in the procreative management of certain birds.

The Spiderhunters (*Arachnothera*) are allied to the Sunbirds. They come from the Far East, and although somewhat larger require much of the same treatment.

Despite their popular appeal, the unique family of tiny nectar-feeding HUMMINGBIRDS are best regarded as specialist material. Only in this way can suitable conditions be provided to them although even then, their breeding will always be difficult.

There are over 300 species—all from the New World—and they vary considerably. The smallest of all (birds) is the Bee Hummingbird which, discounting its beak and tail, is about the size of a bumble bee. The largest is the Giant Hummingbird at more than 20 cm. Their synonimity with jewels and the heavens is illustrated by some of the names man has bestowed upon them: Ruby, Topaz, Sapphire, Emerald, Coronet, Sungem, Sunangel, Hillstar, Comet and Heavenly Sylph.

Much hardier than they look, they enjoy a certain amount of exposure even to rain and snow providing they always have warm, dry quarters to retire to. Indeed, hummingbirds are characterized by a pugnacious intolerance to other small birds especially other hummingbirds, even in large well planted enclosures. Generally speaking, hummingbirds do well so long as things are exactly right but they are prone to failure if conditions are even slightly wrong. Plenty of feeding stations must be provided if there is more than one bird—some tubes being hung in concealed places. Hummingbirds consume several times their own weight in food every day, and their nectar must be augmented by fruit-flies.

At night some species become torpid, thus conserving energy. As with sunbirds bathing should be encouraged by daily spraying or moistened foliage. Their mastery of the air is astonishing; they defy capture by net and invariably leave one looking and feeling stupid. It is no exaggeration to say that they see the net coming and much faster than the eye can follow suddenly appear elsewhere. They can fly backwards, upwards and downwards with equal aplomb; wings beating at 50–80 beats per second give the birds unique advantages which are otherwise possessed only by insects.

Hummingbirds do not differ much in their individual treatment although they do have specific dietary preferences and some are more difficult to establish than others. Possibly the best species to begin with are the *Colibri* violet-ears of which the Sparkling and Brown Violet-eared is an example, or the monotypic Ruby-topaz Hummingbird and the *Amazilia* emerald hummingbirds.

Also called sugarbirds, the New World HONEYCREEPERS (*Emberizidae*) are less dependent on nectar than the hummingbirds and sunbirds but it remains their staple diet—sweet fruit finely diced or simply laid open can be added to it. Honeycreepers can be thought of as tanagers modified for a diet of nectar, pollen and insects. Although they appreciate being allowed to fly about outside during the daytime, they should be allowed to roost inside. Despite being slightly less tough than the sunbirds, they are really no bother to keep and much less quarrelsome.

The male Red-legged Honeycreeper or Yellow-winged Sugarbird moults after the breeding season into a drab female-like eclipse plumage. This species and the Purple or Yellow-legged Honeycreeper are the two most frequently imported. All sugarbirds and other small nectivores require attention at least twice a day. If kept in small cages, these must be cleaned out daily and the perches scrubbed for if this is neglected, the birds soon become soiled owing to the sticky consistency of their droppings which are expelled with some force.

The shorter beak of the little Blue Sugarbird or Dacnis is accurately indicative of a diet containing more fruit and insects. Related but seen less often are the flower-piercers or diglossas (after their generic name) and the Bananaquit. Most are sociable, but an exception is the male Black-headed Honeycreeper which is dangerous to other males and small birds.

Of all nectivorous softbills in captivity, the most difficult to keep are the plump little FLOWERPECKERS from SE Asia. They are not exported frequently, which may be as well since they are only suited to the more experienced keeper. Out of well over 50 species, only the Scarlet-backed and Orange-bellied Flowerpeckers are available from time to time. They need warm planted quarters, plus a broadly based diet which can be divided into finely diced fruit before noon and nectar afterwards since this system has been proved successful.

INSECTIVORES

The British THRUSHES are all good subjects, especially for the beginner. As a whole, the large Muscicapidae family is one of the most popular and representatives are widely available. Breeding is a distinct possibility especially in densely planted accommodation. The Song Thrush and Blackbird are both accomplished songsters, and in the opinion of many people, the latter's song is at least equal to the Nightingale's—which is also a member of this family.

To encourage thrushes to carry their nesting drive through to a successful conclusion, a variety of dried grasses, twigs, rootlets, moss and mud (for some species) has to be provided, followed up by an inexhaustible supply of livefood if eggs should hatch. With indigenous British birds, the provision of food is less difficult, since much can be gleaned from your own neighbourhood: snails, beetles, worms and small slugs apart from the usual maggots and mealworms.

An Asiatic species, the Orange-headed Ground Thrush is one of the commoner exotic thrushes. As its name implies, it is a terrestrial bird and loves to pick through leaf mould. It is generally peaceful but does not get on well with other ground birds. A fine songster, it is as easy to look after as the British thrushes, and like them enjoys bathing.

The Blue-headed Thrush and Chestnut-bellied Rock Thrush are also imported from time to time. Unlike the larger Blue Whistling Thrush which can only be housed with equally robust types, they are fairly friendly.

Allied to the wide-ranging Turninae family which numbers over 300 species are some of the most popular of all insectivores in

Kookaburra

White rumped shama

Grey hooded kingfisher

Carmine bee-eater

Blue winged pitta

aviculture. The small *Copsychus* genus of chat-thrushes contains two of the most famous: White-rumped Shama and the Dhyal Bird or Magpie Robin. The Shama is justly famous for its exceptional voice—which is unusual among chat-thrushes—and is in many ways an ideal bird for the novice softbill keeper except that like its close relatives, it can be territorially aggressive. Almost as popular, the Magpie Robin requires similar standard care and is very tough—both revel in winter conditions providing there is sufficient exercise space. Breeding consists of much torrid activity and a large well planted aviary is needed if only to allow the female some breathing space. Like so many of the commoner softbills, these two handsome birds are Asian in origin.

There are several more minor groups affiliated to the chat-thrushes: bush-robins, bush-chats, robin-chats, redstarts and blue-chats; we need not bother about their subtle demarcations here as some are only popular individually. Almost without exception they are highly territorial, pugnacious little birds originating from the Old World, and it is asking for trouble to mix any species with smaller or similarly-sized softbills, especially if they are terrestrial.

A good example of the bush-robins is the Siberian or Common Rubythroat—a skulking terrestrial bird most active at dusk when its strange frog-like callnote is uttered. The fact that it is in the same genus as the Nightingale (*Luscinia*) unfortunately belies its vocal abilities. The African robin-chats are a trifle more omnivorous than the Asian bush-robins. Notable representatives are the White-browed, Red-capped and Snowy-headed Robin-chats. Characterized by their engaging personalities, robin-chats are rufous birds with bluey-grey wings and, quite often, black and white head-markings.

The song-babblers are more properly located within the omnivorous section but their relatives, the SCIMITAR-BABBLERS, despite consuming a small amount of berries and fruit are basically insectivores. A long curved beak gives them a rather ferocious appearance which in fact is quite opposite to their true and rather shy nature. They are quite hardy, present few problems of management and mix well with their own kind which is just as well seeing they display no sexual dimorphism. One of the best known is the Slaty-headed Scimitar-babbler. Of the 'ordinary' BABBLERS, the Common Babbler from the Far East is a good example of these normally friendly beginners' softbills. Once acclimatized all they ask is a varied insectivorous diet and dry draughtproof roosting quarters.

The purely insectivorous FLYCATCHERS are not for the tyro. They are prone to various weaknesses and can suddenly expire for no apparent reason. Drowning or at least succumbing to chills and pneumonia after getting too wet from bathing—which they love—is a very real hazard; and it is no exaggeration to say that any pool or dish accessible to them should have no more than 1 cm of water in it.

Although difficult to establish initially, the Niltavas are probably the most trouble-free species once 'meated-off', but only the Rufous-bellied Niltava is regularly seen. Otherwise the Tickell's and Verditer Flycatchers are fairly reliable, and can be kept for long periods provided they can be tempted on to a broad-based diet of fine softfood, a variety of livefood including, if possible, flying insects such as maggots which have been allowed to pupate and hatch into blowflies or houseflies. The Asiatic Paradise Flycatcher despite its exquisite beauty should on balance be avoided. Among the African flycatchers, none is frequently available, and such types as the wattle-eyes and puff-backs are only suitable for the professional or specialist; in fact, they are hardly suitable even for them.

Probably the most beautiful of all terrestrial softbills, the PITTAS or 'jewel thrushes' need accommodation which takes into account their ground-living habits: cage bottoms should have a thick layer of moistened peat but their ideal accommodation is a roomy well-planted aviary with an earth floor and drifts of leaf mould. They build intricate globular nests low-down in thick cover and must be given various logs and boulders to perch on. They are mainly insectivorous. While not being difficult to keep, they are territorial and pugnacious to any other ground bird or indeed other small birds when they venture down to ground level.

They do not seem to be exported as much as in the past, and of those which do enter the country, the Blue-winged, Indian or Bengal Pitta is the most reasonably priced.

Numbered amongst the most splendid of all birds—not just softbills—the wide-ranging Coraciiformes and predominantly insectivores made up with just a few carnivorous species such as some of the kingfishers. The following six categories all belong to the Coraciiformes.

The ROLLERS from the Old World are prime examples of the

splendour of these birds and it is unfortunate that their behaviour makes them unsuitable for aviary life. Not that there is any problem in the day to day maintenance—indeed, they are hardy, long-lived, easy to establish and feed on a standard insectivorous diet—it is their quarrelsome attitude towards each other (not surprisingly other species—to which they are more often on the receiving end) and their preference for fathoms of flying space in which they can avoid their own mates outside the breeding season and indulge in the superb flight of the true insect-hawker. Since quite obviously these conditions can seldom be provided in captivity, rollers are unhappy to keep and unlikely to breed. In the unlikely event that breeding is attempted, they would require a nestbox placed as high as possible. The Indian Blue and Lilac-breasted Rollers are the two most often seen, the European Roller less so.

MOTMOTS from the neotropics are in many respects ideal aviary softbills: large, tough once acclimatized, long-lived and fascinating in looks, manner and habits. They have few flaws, perhaps a potential danger to smaller birds is one but it must be said that their powerful serrated beak, physique and somewhat evil aspect is not borne out by their actual behaviour and they seem quite content to sit quietly and watch the world go by, swinging their long tail from side to side like a pendulum. I would, however, still hesitate before housing them with birds very much smaller.

The Blue-crowned Motmot is one that is sometimes met with in some of the better collections. Perhaps the most distinctive feature of motmot management is their need to excavate their own nesting burrows in several feet of earth; given this facility, motmots seem quite willing to breed if a true pair can be formed. It is best to provide an earth bank since this discourages them from tunnelling vertically down—which can create problems of flooding and even escape. Although primarily insectivores, motmots will take larger prey if it happens along.

Like their distant American relatives, the motmots, the Old World BEE-EATERS also nest in earth burrows, but they are less robust and despite a few successes in recent years, bee-eaters are still not suitable aviary inhabitants due to their hawking instincts which they seem loathe to forego and which make them reluctant to accept an adequate substitute diet. Maggots and mealworms alone are insufficient and extensive use of additives is necessary if free-flying insects cannot be provided as for flycatchers. Furthermore, any shortage of insects has rather more rapid and dire consequences than it does with, say, the Hoopoe—another exclusive but more robust insectivore.

For all that, some bee-eaters are seen in specialist collections and the bigger zoos: the Cinnamon-chested, Little and, in recent years, even the marvellous Carmine Bee-eater being the most familiar. The larger species have the unfortunate habit of chasing small birds as if they were insects, and so once again, some softbills have to be carefully mixed with similarly-sized, non-aggressive birds, and birds, moreover, which will not pinch all the bee-eaters' more appetising food in preference to their own!

Widespread across the Old World, the monotypic HOOPOE is a surprisingly trouble-free insectivore which in well-mated pairs proves to be a prolific breeder. Sexes are alike which complicates matters but it is a friendly gregarious species even when nesting— for which it likes a nestbox or some other hole. Given an ad lib supply of live maggots and mealworms, mixed in an insectile-mix fortified with extra vitamins A and D, it is not difficult to keep in excellent condition. While young can be reared successfully on a similar diet, extra minerals must be supplied if they are not to emerge deformed.

Bearing only a superficial resemblance in shape to the Hoopoe, the African WOOD-HOOPOES are mainly dark plumaged birds. They are much more arboreal than the rather terrestrial Hoopoe, equally insectivorous but seldom available to aviculture. Of the eight species, the Green and White-headed Wood-hoopoes are most often encountered.

Peaceful in their relations to other birds, wood-hoopoes do well in large aviaries equipped with a high nestbox with smallish entrance hole—in which they will roost and also spend much of the day simply peering out or hiding altogether. One of the main disadvantages I have found with wood-hoopoes is their habit of excreting while circling the aviary in flight; this has the annoying effect of spraying all vegetation, wire and walls with unpleasant white decorations.

KINGFISHERS by and large are misnamed—most are forest or upland birds living on terrestrial fauna; many are in fact more insectivorous than carnivorous, but most thrive on a diet of livefood and slim strips of fish and meat placed in a secure dish of water. Spacious pools are necessary if only for bathing purposes (see also TYRANT FLYCATCHERS).

Kingfishers are either tree-nesters· or burrowers but like practically all the Coraciiformes make exclusive use of holes. The Woodland Kingfisher bred successfully at the Winged World in an artificial earth bank. Apart from this vigorous African species, other suitable avicultural subjects are the White-breasted, Grey-hooded and Senegal Kingfishers. The last two mentioned are also African while the White-breasted originate from the Far East; all are peaceful and far less trouble than might be imagined, although they can be troublesome to other birds which are nesting. Some of the smallest species, like the Malachite and Pygmy Kingfishers are highly attractive and while they can be kept in captivity successfully, are really only suitable for the more experienced amateur and professional. The Kookaburra is one of the most carnivorous species—famous for its call—but seldom available since Australia instituted strict export laws.

Similarly, WOODPECKERS are avoided by most amateurs on account of their exclusively insectivorous food requirements; the fact that they are notoriously difficult to 'meat-off' results in a high price. Other disadvantages are their argumentative natures and the fact that they are quite unbelievably destructive to all accessible woodwork. On the credit side are their engaging personalities, hardiness and longevity once established. The Golden-backed Woodpecker and its cogeners from India and surrounding areas are the most commonly seen species in British collections.

The TITMICE are often neglected but in fact make delightful and rewarding occupants for well-planted aviaries. The Indian Green-backed Tit can be obtained at a very reasonable price: it and similar types are perky, dainty, highly active and not in the least difficult to maintain on a good insectile-mix, livefood and just a little seed and nuts. If a true pair can be obtained, (which is not easy as the sexes are alike) and a suitable nestbox provided, there is no good reason why they should not breed. The tropical species such as this should always have access to warm dry quarters in the winter although they are probably quite hardy once established.

NUTHATCHES are fairly rare in collections, the Chestnut-bellied Nuthatch occurring in India and eastwards, being the best known. They display boundless energy, racing around from tree to tree and burning up their insectivorous food at an alarming speed. They are ultimately quite hardy but very territorial and difficult to breed needing small nestboxes or well-hidden crannies. Management very similar to the titmice.

The Asiatic MINIVETS are members of the cuckoo-shrike family—highly insectivorous and very beautiful but expensive and in demand only from elitist collectors. The Scarlet and, to a lesser extent, the Orange Minivet occasionally reach these shores from India. Males are more colourful than the females which, as is often the case, are less frequently exported. Minivets are gregarious, arboreal and of a peaceful disposition unlike the true SHRIKES which are aggressive, fairly carnivorous and even more infrequently imported.

CUCKOO is a name given to many members of the large Cuculidae family but it covers a wide range of species. Cuckoos are indeed mainly parasitic; the non-parasitic sorts are called coucals, malcohas and koels. The smaller cuckoos are extremely insectivorous in taste and contain many desirable species such as the Klaas' and Emerald Cuckoos although none of this family can be said to be common in captivity.

The larger representatives are considerably more aggressive: their strong stout beaks plainly capable of much damage to smaller birds. Although seldom imported, the malcohas are seen in some of the better collections; they are non-parasitic, less arboreal as their alternative name 'ground-cuckoos' suggests and enjoy large insects such as locusts, cockroaches, invertebrates and even small vertebrates and some fruit. Again, they are really in the domain of the specialist.

Other species of insectivorous softbills too numerous to mention individually are also sometimes kept. Quite often these appear as 'one-off' importations and are not generally successful in the long term. In this book I have had to limit myself to the standard species but among those which can sometimes be acquired are trogons, oxpeckers, wrens, rails, mockingbirds, roadrunners, longclaws, drongoes and the unusual Sunbittern from the Amazon basin. For particulars of these and more, reference should be made to more specialized works, field guides and such like. It beholds all of us of course to learn as much as we can from all possible sources about ALL our birds. The study of softbills remains exciting and their aviculture challenging.

Index